Betsy Bell

## About the Author

JEFF KREISLER is a graduate of Exeter, Princeton, and Virginia Law School; a writer for Comedy Central's Indecision2008 and 236.com; and a winner of the Bill Hicks Spirit Award for Thought Provoking Comedy. He has a political comedy tour (Comedy Against Evil) and a humor column, is executive editor of the parody *My Wall Street Journal*, created the critically acclaimed live sitcom *The Americans*, has performed with presidential candidates, is in the cast of *Shoot the Messenger* (from the cocreator of *The Daily Show*), had hit shows at the Edinburgh Fringe and Glasgow comedy festivals, and was featured on the BBC, BBC-America, and Current TV, as well as CBS, NPR, and Sirius radio networks. He was an all-league college football player; taught English in Russia; started a nonprofit dedicated to at-risk youth; plays mediocre blues on the alto sax; has lived in New York City, San Francisco, Boston, and D.C.; and loves asparagus.

www.JeffKreisler.com
www.GetRichCheating.com.

# Get Rich
# **Cheating**

# Get Rich
# **Cheating**

## THE CR00KED PATH TO EASY STREET

### Jeff Kreisler

<u>HARPER</u>

NEW YORK · LONDON · TORONTO · SYDNEY

## HARPER

HarperCollins books may be purchased for educational, business, or sales promotional use. For information please write: Special Markets Department, HarperCollins Publishers, 10 East 53rd Street, New York, NY 10022.

FIRST EDITION

*Designed by Joy O'Meara*

Library of Congress Cataloging-in-Publication Data is available upon request.

ISBN 978-0-06-168614-6

09 10 11 12 13   OV/RRD   10 9 8 7 6 5 4 3 2 1

*To money, the root of all good*

# Contents

# Contents

## Part III: What If You're Caught?

# Introduction

You are poor. No matter what you do, where you live, whom you love, or even how much money you have, you are poor. Very poor. Poor, poor, *poor*.

You've lost your home, your 401k, your pension, your thirty-five-inch high-def plasma TV-Xbox-iPhone-SUV, and your will to live. You need more money. You *want* more money. Badly. *Now.*

But we're in a "financial crisis," a "recession," a "serious bummer." Things are bad: markets have collapsed, banks have folded, and Britney's staged another comeback. *Mercy!* How can you possibly get all the money you want in these tough times?

You need help. You need hope. You need to cheat.

Even now, there are tons of cheaters making gigantic fortunes. *Million*-dollar contracts! *Billion*-dollar bonuses! *Trillion*-dollar bailouts! Some get suspended, fired, or arrested and *still* pull down six, seven, eight figures while awaiting trial in their Manhattan penthouses. How do they do it? They cheat. Look at inspiring examples like Barry Bonds, Paris Hilton, Rod Blagojevich, and corporate cheaters like Ken Lay, Bernie Madoff, Fannie Mae, AIG, and the omni-businesswoman extraordinaire, your friend and mine, the iconic Caucasian American female entrepreneur, Martha Stewart, a.k.a. White Oprah!

Until now, you thought of people like them as "corporate criminals," "juiced athletes," "spoiled stars," or "scumbag politicians." From this moment forward, you'll revere them as "Great Cheaters." Don't you want to be like them? To have their money, respect, and power? They Got Rich Cheating. You can too. This book will show you how.

*Get Rich Cheating* offers practical advice for the aspiring cheat. In the pages that follow, you'll uncover the secret methods of the Great Cheaters. By the end, you'll have gathered all their proven wealth-creation techniques. There will be facts, figures, exaggerations, examples, suggestions, and a few pretty pictures. You'll learn, you'll laugh, you'll cry, you'll gasp in horror, but most of all you *will* Get Rich Cheating.

By just picking up this book, you've already done more than most people dare. Congratulations, my new friend. This moment will change your life. Embrace it, savor it, and inhale deeply the musk of your impending wealth.

Let's Get Rich Cheating.

# How to Use This Book

Part I, Why Cheat?, introduces the idea of cheating for wealth, its history, its benefits, and why this is the perfect time and the perfect place to be a cheater.

Part II, How to Cheat, presents awesome ideas from the Great Cheaters, as well as examples, commentary, suggestions, and scenarios. Learn from them and copy them. The Feds would never think you'd be that dumb.

Part III, What If You're Caught?, explains that even if you follow the advice in Part II—well, *especially* if you follow that advice—there's a slight chance you might get caught. What then? How do you prepare, whom do you bribe, what do you wear? If worse comes to worst, there's always faking death and vacationing with Elvis and Jimmy Hoffa.

It's tragic when a CEO, ballplayer, politician, or starlet simply retires without controversy, when companies remain solvent, communities happy, investors satisfied, and the Feds unconcerned. Opportunity has been wasted. Great Cheaters avoid this waste and turn circumstance into fortune. You'll read about their experiences, in their own distorted words, in a series of Succes$tories, In$pirations, and Le$$ons. Go ahead, write those down. They're trademarked, so every time you use them, you owe me a dollar.

# How to Use This Book

*What this book is not*: It's not another get-rich-quick scam. If you're looking for an elusive, impossible, overnight fortune, look elsewhere. The techniques in this book will require months, even *weeks*, to pay off.

*Get Rich Cheating* will provide ideas; the execution is up to you. Fortune awaits—if you're serious about cheating. It's impossible for you to fail.* So hitch your wagon to the Get Rich Cheating money train. Destination: You.

---

* Not a guarantee.

# Part I

# Why Cheat?

# Part 1

# Why Cheat?

# I

## Why Not?

### And Why Not *You?*

Are the Great Cheaters better than you? *Of course not.* They just know one thing you don't: Cheating is the quickest, surest, most glorious path to everlasting wealth.

Have you ever cheated? On your expense report, your golf score, your wife? *Of course you have.* Why not get rich doing it?

Despite the "recession," there are still trillions of dollars flowing through the global economy. You can have some, but only if you take action. Ed McMahon's not going to show up at your door with a van full of balloons and a giant $200 million novelty check. You've got to get off the couch, get yourself together, and Get Rich Cheating.

What are your current plans for building wealth? A job? Investments? The lottery? Waiting for Grandma to die? Stocks give you, maybe, a 10 percent return. A career? *Yeah, like anyone ever bought a yacht off a salary.* Even get-rich-quick real estate schemes only promise, like, $1 million in five years. *That's "rich" "quick"?* You might as well beg for change on the corner of Loser Street and Failure Lane.

Most of those schemes involve research, time, and effort. Get Rich Cheating is quicker, easier, and more fun. Instead of $1 million in five years, how about *$500* million in *one* year, $25 million to make a movie, or $210 million to hit baseballs? With cheating, you'll get a 300 percent, 40,000 percent, 50 million percent return on your investment. *Guaranteed.**

Why not cheat? Everyone's doing it: athletes, entertainers, politicians, and big-business executives. They use steroids, plastic surgery, lip-synching, accounting scams, backdoor deals, computerized voting machines, and more. They've all gone down the proven path of deceit, lies, and treachery that leads to money, fame, and glory. You can, too, and you can do it better than them. I'll help.

**CHEAT CHAT**

"Who are you?"

I get that a lot. Not long ago, I was just like you, an average guy, your neighborhood "Joe the Plumber," trying to make it big. I had all the prerequisites to acquire

---

\*   Not a guarantee.

wealth through a traditional career: I went to Princeton, I had a law degree (so when I say, "Trust me, I'm a lawyer," you really should trust me . . . because I'm a lawyer), I had a friend who knew a guy at this place that did some stuff. I also lacked a desire to work hard, an ability to sacrifice, and any concept of morality or ethics. Fortunately, I needed none of those to Get Rich Cheating.

I diligently studied the exploits of the Great Cheaters. I learned how they made their millions: without skill, without grace, without integrity, and, above all, without anything but a simple desire to make themselves as wealthy as possible, and to do so before anyone realized what they'd done.

So who am I? I am a man who knows the way of the Great Cheater, and I will impart my knowledge to you. I am your teacher, guide, guru, and sensei, your cheerleader, champion, and number one fan. I am here to help you. Trust me, I'm a lawyer.

Cheating is defined by poor-people dictionaries as "deception by trickery, fraud, and dishonesty." Not here. This is a safe place, without judgments or preconceived notions of "right" and "wrong." Cheating is broadly defined by the Cheaters English Dictionary (CED) as "Awesome personal gain by means that are illegal, immoral, and fun."

*"But Jeff, cheating seems wrong."*

Does it, friend? Well, it's not wrong, nor is it "bad," nor will it send you to Hell. *It won't.* Wipe that idea right out of your head. That's just hippie talk, programmed into you by a weak culture that doesn't want *you* to succeed. Let me tell you, cheating is *great*, and doing it well will make you a *Great* Cheater. Sure, some Great Cheaters went to jail, but that's just a speed bump on the road to riches.

Let me dispel a myth right now: We're *not* "all in this together." There's no "we" in "rich." A rising tide may lift all boats, but only an inch or two. A geyser of focused cheating can blast *you* and *your* expensive boat to unimagined heights of ecstasy and wealth.

Why cheat? Simple: Money. Money. *Money.*

This is why you do it, why you're in the game. The minimum wage is $6.55. *Per hour!* Do you realize how many hours you'd have to "work" to get as much money as you can cheat in a single day? A lot! Probably more than ten!

Work? *No, thank you.*

Cheat? *Yes, please.*

As you think about how much you should be earning, it's important to consider what the other cheaters around you earn. Your cash starts at their baseline because of a simple word that will change your life: "benchmark." Comparing earnings within your industry to establish your own pay. With benchmarking, your income doesn't have to do with competence or ability; it just has to do with what your peers get. For instance, the franchise tag in the NFL means a player gets the average salary of the top five players at his position, MLB arbitration hearings compare similar players, and on and on. Who sets your pay? *Your peers.* Who sets their pay? *Their peers.* Who are their peers? *You.* Who sets your pay? *Your peers.* Like Elton John sang in *The Lion King*: It's the Circle of Wealth.

**CHEAT CHAT**

On benchmarking: Be jealous. If someone's making $6 million, you should make $7 million; you make $7 million, they'll want $8 million; they make $8 million, you'll demand $9 million; and so on, et cetera, *ad infinitum.* Call it "The Free Market" . . . because that sounds better than "Incestuous Self-Bidding."

Since it just takes one to set the standard, it's already pretty high. How high? Consider the take of some Great Cheaters in some cheating industries.

## Bidne$$

In the three years before Enron collapsed, twenty-nine executives made more than $1 billion in stock sales. In 2007, the *average* CEO of an S&P 500 company made $14.2 million per year in total compensation. You're not average, you're a cheater. CEOs at companies *under investigation* earned 70 percent more than other CEOs.* Considering what you're about to do, an "investigative raise" is guaranteed.

Remember that $6.55 minimum wage? Henry Kravis of Kohlberg Kravis Roberts made $450 million in 2006—that's $1.3 million per day, over $51,000 per hour. Richard Fuld earned $45 million in 2007 while destroying Lehman Brothers. That's $17,000 per hour. *Ahem. Which is better, minimum wage or cheating wage? Hmmm.*

If you've still got cold feet, look at this mostly true chart:

## CEO TO AVERAGE WORKER SALARY RATIO

1980 — 42:1
1990 — 85:1
2000 — 531:1
2050 — 140,000,000:1 (projected)

You don't want to be another worker bee. You want to be the queen bee, buzzing around a hive full of money.

## $ports

Barry Bonds has career earnings—from salary alone—of about $188 million. Roger Clemens: around $133 million. Mark McGwire: in the neighborhood of $75 million. That's

---

* That was back in 2001. I'm *so totally sure* it's even better now.

a nice neighborhood, despite all the guys with gigantic heads.

If you just cheat into the big leagues, you'll do okay, too. The average salary of an NFL player is just over $2 million. The *minimum* is between $285,000 and $820,000, depending on how long you've cheated, a.k.a. "been in the pros." The MLB minimum is $400,000, and the *average* salary is over $3 million. The NBA minimum ranges from $400,000 to $1.3 million, and the average in Hoopsville is $5.8 million. That's a lot of palimony checks.

College sports pay well, too . . . *for coaches*. College football: $950,000 plus perks. Basketball: $800,000 and up. Oklahoma's Mike Stoops got $6 million in one year. Considering he's following in the Great Cheater footsteps of Barry Switzer, I'm sure he's earned every penny . . . the Get Rich Cheating way. All that money, just to coach "football," or what the British call "sweet racket!"

The best thing about getting rich college-coach style is that your players do all the work for you. You get loaded off of their blood, sweat, and years. They get nothing—no back-end deals, performance bonuses, or speaker fees. They have to show up and work every day for free because they're getting a "university degree." *Ha!* When was the last time someone bought tickets on a Russian spaceship with a "degree?" Coaches 1, Athletes 0.

## $how Bu$iness

Entertainers make money hand over fist over fake boob over casting couch. There's the endorsement bonanza, from Celine Dion's fourteen million Chrysler dollars to Catherine Zeta-Jones's $20 million from T-Mobile to the guy who played Screech on *Saved by the Bell* getting fifty bucks from me to please, please go away.

Then there's the "regular" pay a cheater makes in showbiz. Lindsay Lohan has a $7.5 million salary; Paris Hilton makes upwards of $15 million for TV, movies, modeling, and personal appearances; Britney Spears made tens of millions on tour; the cast of *Friends* pulled in $1 million per drivel-filled episode; Paul McCartney is worth about $1 billion; and stars from Tom Cruise to Julia Roberts to George Clooney make $15, $20, and $25 million just to appear in a single movie.

Keep in mind that while, technically, these folks are "working," their "jobs" entail very little—*smile, repeat these words, don't get hit by a truck*—and so get filed under cheating. The question you should be asking is not, "*Why do we call these celebrities cheaters?*" but "*Why don't I have a head shot?*"

## Politic$

Becoming an elected official gets you not just decent pay, but great retirement benefits, consulting and speaker fees, and the right of *primae noctis* in much of the South. George W. Bush got himself $400,000 a year in salary while "working" as president. Once out of office, he joined the likes of Bill Clinton and the elder Bush in pulling in million-dollar taxpayer-funded retirement payments, even though most former presidents were rich before they came into office. The rich get richer, the cheats get cheater.

Bill and Hillary Clinton earned $109 million in 2007, mostly from books, speaker fees, and the residual payments from that "vast right-wing conspiracy." Rudy Giuliani, the former mayor of New York, made $9.2 million on a speaking tour in 2006 and 2007. Speaking about what? Who cares? The man's getting paid big bucks to flap his gums for forty minutes. Need I say more?

That's just a few elected officials. We haven't even touched upon the money earned by lobbyists, contractors, call girls, and others connected to cheating politicians. There's so much money to cheat in politics, they even have a name for it: the Federal Budget.

$ $ $

Still not sold on the idea that cheating is the right path for you? Just remember that money buys everything. It's still a gilded age, with VIP lounges, admirals' clubs, first class, bottle service, and gated communities on every corner. Possession is nine-tenths of the law, and, according to TV, *possessions* are nine-tenths of our value as human beings. Your worth is tied to your wealth, your being based upon your bling. Whoever dies with the most stuff wins.

When you Get Rich Cheating, your material possessions have extra value. They'll be infused with an element of danger because of the risks you took to get them. That bearskin rug you bought with proceeds from your steroid-aided, gold-medal-winning breakfast cereal sponsorship . . . *it could have killed you*. You're a cheater breaking the rules, a rebel living on the edge. You deserve the best. Don't think of your possessions as "things." Think of them as "loot," or "booty," or "*ill-gotten* booty" from your pirate adventures on deceitful seas.

Frankly, when you Get Rich Cheating, you have a *duty* to flaunt your success, an obligation to those who adore you. The Little Leaguers, five-year-old beauty queens, high school class presidents, and momma's-basement-bound day traders with a precarious grasp on hope. Great Cheaters are their heroes, the rock stars of the twenty-first century. When you Get Rich Cheating, your devotees will follow your financial expenditures the way fans in days gone by followed the box scores of Mantle and Mays. Your admirers will even make excuses *for you*, like San Franciscans do for Barry Bonds. You'll be their star, and you'll have to live up to that every day. Excess will be your burden.

**In$piration:** *"It's the type of lifestyle that's difficult to turn on and off like a spigot."*
—Ken Lay, testifying before a jury[*]

Think about your fans, the little kids who spend hours in front of a mirror, pretending to inject a needle into their buttocks, stuffing their bra, taking bribes from their siblings,

---

[*] Really.

practicing their "who me?" face, and dreaming of initiating a mass layoff. Keep your eyes on the prize: money and the things it will buy. Smother yourself in stuff.

Previous cheaters have done plenty with their money. *I bet you can do better.*

- **Dennis Kozlowski:** A $6,000 shower curtain? *Amateur. For you, a $6,000 loofah.*
- **Same guy:** A $2 million birthday party for his wife on Sardinia. *You can spend that much on the invitations.*
- **Still Koz:** $15,000 on an umbrella stand shaped like a French poodle. *Couldn't he afford to train real poodles to hold his rainwear?*
- **P. Diddy** has a million-dollar watch. *If he were really rich, he wouldn't have to be on time.*
- **Conrad Black** spent $9 million of Hollinger's funds to purchase FDR's presidential papers, *because he didn't have the nerve to buy Truman's.*
- **Lil' Kim** has a coat made of squirrel and chinchilla. *Because "Lil'" refers to her spending imagination: She couldn't find an endangered species to relieve of its heavy winter jacket?*
- **Stephen Hilbert** of Conseco built a replica of Indiana University's Assembly Hall basketball court. *Hello? What about cloning the school's best players to re-create exciting games?*

You've probably got your own ideas about what you need,

what you want, what you might get. Here's a short list of suggested purchases, inspired by the Great Cheaters:

Houses. Everywhere.
Servants with British accents
The love of a good woman
The love of several mediocre women
The NYC mayor's office
The Sharper Image catalog, pages 2–74
Yes-men
Yes-women
Yes, the band
Dodo-bird filet
Fabergé Egg omelets
White rhino soufflé
Statues, plaques, honorary degrees
Adjunct professorships
Oral Roberts University
The Oakland Raiders
A pony

As you can see, money has its upside. It's not just for rent and food and alimony anymore. Sometimes it's for fun. So go on already—Get Rich Cheating. If you cheat yourself enough money, you'll live forever. Just ask Ted Turner.

**2**

## A Brief History of Cheating

### From Eve to Enron

There is a grand, historic tradition of cheating for riches. After all, the "oldest profession" is based upon man's desire to cheat on one woman, and another woman's desire to profit from that infidelity. Seems like a fair trade.

From the dawn of time to the instant we're engulfed by the flames of an angry sun, cheating has and will provide mankind with everything it needs. Do not fear, aspiring cheat. Your actions are not without precedent, and you are not without guidance. As you embark upon your noble quest to Get Rich Cheating, remember that you "stand on the shoulders of giants." *If you just bend down, you can steal their ideas.*

| Date | Great Moment in Cheating |
| --- | --- |
| DARKNESS | The Lord creates Heaven and Earth. Works six days, submits invoice for seven. |
| THURSDAY, BC | Serpent removes Adam and Eve from the board of Eden Industries with apple-based poison pill. |

| Date | Great Moment in Cheating |
|------|--------------------------|
| FIFTH CENTURY, BC | Mercury banned from the Olympics for performance-enhancing winged feet. Becomes god of trade, profit, and commerce. Sets sights on career in flower delivery. |
| 1206 | Genghis Khan proposes merger with Asia Inc. Rebuffed, he brutalizes region to build largest contiguous empire in history . . . until Google. |
| 1555 | The Muscovy Company chartered; becomes the first joint-stock trading company. |
| 1556 | The Muscovy Company becomes the first company to defraud investors and give its CEO a gigantic severance package. |
| 1611 | King James steals draft of the Bible from a court jester. Makes millions on movie rights. |
| 1787 | Delaware is first state to ratify the U.S. Constitution. Population of 10,000 includes 9,999 businesses drawn by law allowing corporations to "rape, kill, pillage, and burn." |
| 1789 | Samuel Slater uses stolen technology to build America's first successful cotton mill. Really. |
| 1792 | Merchants and traders establish stock and bond exchange in lower Manhattan. Euphoria spreads across butler and horse-drawn limo industries. |
| 1870s | John D. Rockefeller builds Standard Oil into great monopoly. Once his company is broken up, oil is never again an economic or political issue. Ever. |
| 1919 | Black Sox scandal rocks baseball, makes baseball commissioners and documentary filmmakers rich |

| Date | Great Moment in Cheating |
|---|---|
| | and powerful. Cheating is never again a problem in baseball. Ever. |
| 1926 | SATs introduced. Millions of wealthy Americans learn that Privilege is to Merit as Cheating is to Hard Work. |
| 1929 | Stock market crash engineered by author John Steinbeck in order to boost sales of his forthcoming *The Grapes of Wrath*. |
| 1943 | Fidelity Investments founded, starting great tradition of corporations with names that contradict their business philosophy. |
| 1969 | Moon landing faked under pressure from moon rock industry. Scam revealed when MTV lands on real, kick-ass moon in 1980s. |
| 1969–1989 | Michael Milken frauds his way to riches and fame. A bright star in a dark universe. |
| 1977 | David Berkowitz, a.k.a. "Son of Sam," terrorizes New York City. Writes off dead bodies as "capital expenditures." |
| 1979 | The Devil goes down to Georgia, where he is defeated by a young fiddler named Bill Gates. Devil rewards Gates with concept of bundling software and Windows Vista. |
| 1980s | Results for the Pepsi Challenge are fabricated. A defeated Coca-Cola introduces "New Coke"; never recovers. |
| 1985 | Enron founded. Seed money provided by the private equity firm of Lucifer & Beelzebub. |

| Date | Great Moment in Cheating |
|------|--------------------------|
| 1988 | Ben Johnson wins Olympic gold. Signs lucrative endorsement deals with unusual "No give-backs for steroids" clause. |
| 1993 | Paris Hilton appears in her first movie, *Wishman,* as Girl on Beach. Space-time continuum shudders. |
| 1995 | After Netscape IPO is, technically, "a ludicrous bonanza of undeserved billions," Pets.com is conceived in prison laundry room. |
| 1998 | Mark McGwire hits seventy home runs, grows third arm, places fifth in Kentucky Derby. |
| 1998–2006 | NY Attorney General Eliot Spitzer has permanent dose of caffeine, spends years ruining perfectly good scams for everyone. |
| 2000 | "Votes" are "counted" in "Florida" for "president." |
| 2002 | Sarbanes-Oxley Act signed. Corporate officers now responsible for certifying accounting, finding loopholes. |
| 2003 | Jayson Blair fired for fabricating *New York Times* stories. Makes fortune on book deal, lecture circuit. Is currently laughing at you. |
| 2004 | "Votes" are "counted" in "Ohio" for "president." |
| 2006 | Ken Lay fakes own death, buys timeshare in Ibiza next to Elvis and Hoffa. |
| 2009 | You buy and read *Get Rich Cheating.* |

## 3

# No Time Like the President

*Greed is good.*

—GORDON GEKKO

Twenty-first century America is the perfect place to Get Rich Cheating. American culture is fertile soil; you can be the greedy little weed growing in our garden. Cheating is in. Cheating is hot. Simply put, cheating is just so *now*. Open any publication and read three articles. At least one involves cheating, doesn't it? It is an integral part of popular culture. Who polarizes every reality show? *The cheaters.* Why do people love the women of *Desperate Housewives*? *Because they cheat.* Who's the next high-profile figure to resign in disgrace? *A cheat.*

Your favorite athletes? *Cheats.*

The movie star with the enhanced body parts? *A cheater.*

Oprah's best-selling author? *Cheat-tastic.*

That congressman? *Robert's Rules of Cheating.*

The student in the back row? *Cheat-sheet complete.*

Everyone's doing it. If you don't do it too, you'll be left behind. Your classmates will wreck the curve. Your competitor will steal your customer. Heck, your wife's sleeping with the pool boy, so you might as well knock up the nanny.

Why is America such a great place to cheat? This guy David Callahan wrote a book called *The Cheating Culture: Why More Americans Are Doing Wrong to Get Ahead.** It's really interesting and informative if you like terrible things that are wrong. He's all, like, "Cheating is bad, this is why, we should change things, boo-hoo-hoo, I stubbed my toe and miss my mommy." Hey, David Callahan, every party needs a pooper—that's why we invited you, you turd.

We're a competitive society that places great importance on gaining wealth, while providing few real opportunities to do so. Economic mobility is more myth than reality. We want to be rich and we want it *now*, but unless we're born wealthy or invented YouTube, it's not going to happen.

Have you seen the latest episode of *Lifestyles of the Poor and Decrepit*? No, you haven't, because that show doesn't exist. *Lifestyles of the Rich and Famous*? *MTV Cribs*? *People with More Money Than You Doing Stuff You Can Only Dream About*? They're on every afternoon because Americans value money above all else. Life in America is kill or be killed. Success at all costs. Whether it's the cultural dominance of competitive sports or the pervasive demands to vanquish and humiliate others, there's something wonderful about a six-year-old wearing a T-shirt that says "Win or Go Home"

---

* David Callahan, *The Cheating Culture: Why More Americans Are Doing Wrong to Get Ahead* (Orlando: Harcourt Books, 2004).

instead of displaying a picture of Winnie the Pooh. Come on. Pooh was such a loser, he couldn't even afford pants.

I can't tell you how many times I've watched a little boy whining about the latest Xbox and thought, "There are children starving in Africa, half the globe is embroiled in ethno-religious conflict, and this self-indulgent kid believes he's *owed* a new toy. What a well-reared future cheater!" Americans are just like that little kid. We believe we deserve the best, on our terms, at all times.

So. We. Cheat. Without opportunities to legitimately achieve what we believe we're due, cheating becomes the only way to fulfill our self-created destiny. If we believe it is our divine right to have money, we will do whatever is necessary to get it. The goal of life is to make money; the means don't matter.

Society has changed. Notions of right and wrong are shaped by family, friends, and culture, and those things all now say cheating is okeydokey. It's a self-fulfilling, self-reinforcing, self-serving prophecy that benefits you, the aspiring cheat. We're numb to cheating, numb to steroids, corporate crime, stolen elections, and talentless fame. Every new accomplishment—a track and field record, a huge corporate payout, a TV deal, or an election—brings immediate scrutiny. Everyone assumes there's cheating—even *expects* you to cheat—so why not do it? Right now.

What a great time to be alive! It's the start of another bubble, like the tech bubble of the nineties or the real estate bubble of this decade. It's the cheating bubble. Start blowing, start cheating, start getting rich now.

Now, let's say you're reading this a hundred years in the future and thinking, "I'm worried that if I start cheating now, the bubble will have already burst." *Wrong*. While I don't know what the future looks like exactly, I'm pretty sure I can at least describe the political climate: One of two major parties is in charge, there's partisan bickering, an "illegitimate" president, money plays a key role in the elective process, lobbyists dictate legislative agendas, corruption is widespread, and corporations still control the voting machines. *Nice*.

American political culture simply provides a big green light for those with power and the inclination to cheat. Consider these commonly accepted economic principles of America:

- Aggressive tax cuts to the wealthiest Americans, or "trickle-down economics," which, as you know, is when the rich urinate on the poor.
- Bankrupting the Treasury with needless war(s), so there are no resources to police corporations' bad actions. They're free to renege on promises, dump toxic waste, mass-produce Tickle Me Elmo dolls in a lead-melting plant, and convince people that Britney Spears has talent.
- *Regulation, schmegulation*. Let industry make its own rules. Our energy policy is shaped by energy companies, the Healthy Forests Initiative by logging companies, the Clean Skies Initiative by polluters, the Occupational Safety and Health Administration by no one, Child Protection by Mark Foley.

- "Publicly embrace reform while working diligently behind the scenes to undermine it."*
- *Stubbornness.* Congress wanted to eliminate the estate tax, a.k.a. the Death Tax, which prevents me from passing on my ill-gotten booty to my even less-deserving heirs. After several unsuccessful alternative attempts, they cleverly tied repeal of the Death Tax to raising the minimum wage. When *that* didn't work, the president simply fired the lawyers responsible for enforcing the Death Tax. If at first you don't succeed, cheat, cheat again.
- No one's watching. Even if some enterprising young reporter digs deep, uncovers wrongdoing, and explains it to people in lay terms, the media are so thoroughly discredited that no one will believe it. Heck, in 2007, a federal judge admonished a reporter for helping reveal the dangers of Eli Lilly's drug Zyprexa. Thank you, Judge, for reminding the media of their duties: selling products under the guise of "informing the public."

When thinking about the government's role in our cheating, take a moment to reflect upon the former Commander-in-Cheat, George W. Bush. Although his time is, sadly, done, we must appreciate his example. Even those who irrationally

---

* Arianna Huffington, *Pigs at the Trough* (New York: Crown, 2003). What Little Miss Whiny Foreign Accent Not-So-Clever forgets to mention in her tree-hugging manifesto is that effective regulation would let the terrorists win.

hated the guy admit he's good. He ran unsuccessful baseball and oil companies, made questionable stock trades, schemed his way into the presidency, ran it like a fraudulent corporation, hid his reasons, played dumb, refused to take responsibility, and enriched those around him. He was on a nickname basis with Great Cheater Ken Lay, engaged in confounding doublespeak and nonsensical blathering, and added "signing statements" to laws that allowed him to ignore them. *So good*.

W's people were inspirational too. Vice President Dick Cheney will shoot you in the face. *He will!* His relationships produced everything from no-bid Halliburton contracts to the industry-heavy Energy Task Force. He resolved those potential conflicts of interest by "hunting" with his good pal, Supreme Court Justice Antonin Scalia . . . *if you know what I mean*.

Then there were W's appointees:

- Allan Hubbard, economic advisor to the president, killed off regulations that hindered his own financial interests.
- Michael Leavitt, secretary of Health and Human Services, proposed new rules to regulate safety for workers, parts of which were lifted *verbatim* from coal industry suggestions.
- Former Treasury Secretary Paul O'Neill, Secretary of Commerce Donald Evans, Office of Management and

Budget chief Mitch Daniels, and Armed Forces heads Thomas White, James Roche, and Gordon England all ran companies whose success was based solely on regulatory approvals, cartel-like behavior, or government contracts.

- Grinch, undersecretary for Stealing Christmas, pushed through an anti-Santa tax that disproportionately benefited the naughty.

George W. Bush didn't just Get *Rich* Cheating, he got *totally awesome* cheating. He was the rootinest, tootinest CEO of the biggest, baddest, most cheatingest company there is: America.

You are a patriot, and when you Get Rich Cheating, you too will make America stronger, safer, and more free.

# 4

## No One's Going to Stop You

### Really

Worried about getting caught cheating? Don't be. Who's going to catch you? The underfunded SEC or politically corrupt Department of Justice? *Nah.* Employees, team owners, advertisers, programmers, studios, or investors who all have a financial stake in your success? *Yeah, right.* Attorneys general whom you've appointed? *No, sir.* Superman? *Not if your kryptonite money belt does its job.*

Within each industry, the police powers are more interested in protecting the members of their group than in protecting the members of society. Now and then they'll carry out a high-profile bust just to keep the public satisfied—after all, it's hard to eat doughnuts with someone on your back—but that's it.

## Athletic Supporter

The drug-testing regimes in major sports are a joke. Yeah, sure, doping is "outlawed" and every few years owners and player reps get dragged in front of Congress to pretend to lament the bad example doped-up athletes are setting for little Billy, but, well, Billy's not *your* kid, so Billy and his mutations can fend for themselves.

Sports are tremendously lucrative businesses. Football, baseball, basketball, hockey, soccer, track and field, cycling, tennis, beach volleyball, pro wrestling, and co-ed naked badminton are cash machines pumping zillions of dollars into the pockets of cheaters everywhere. There are ticket sales and TV deals, merchandising, sponsorship, and hero worship. Last year alone, the NFL made somewhere between an assload and a buttload: Technically, it's known as "a taintload."

Sports leagues and broadcasting networks have a $imple incentive to look the other way on cheating. Revenue is driven by high performance, drama, and excitement. What's more exciting than seeing if some pituitary freak can smash five hundred home runs before his head explodes? *Nothing*. Modern sports are also about individual stars, and your star can only shine brightly if you cheat. No one pays $10,000 for a personal seat license just to watch fat Uncle Lou wheeze across the fifty-yard line.

As far as the leagues are concerned, the real crime isn't doing drugs—it's the hassle of dealing with an athlete who gets caught. NFL players who violate drug policy get suspended for just four games so they can get back out there and smash in some brains. Beating dogs brings a much stiffer penalty, and they can't even throw a spiral.

Even if they wanted to, the sports authorities could never catch you. In college sports, unless it's point-fixing or gambling, it's all totally "legal." Ever heard of NCAA jail? No, otherwise Bobby Knight would've shivved UNLV in Division II Oz long ago. The NFL and MLB can do what they want because they have congressional antitrust exemptions. The motivated-by-money athletic pharmacist and bathing suit designer will always be several steps ahead of the no-incentive police. If they can clone a sheep, why can't you clone Mark McGwire's arms? So inject, collude, exploit, and swing away.

## Mind Your Own Show Business

Is there a "governing body" responsible for enforcing "ethical behavior" in Hollywood? Does using the phrase "ethical behavior" in the same sentence as "Hollywood" make me eligible for an industry award? *The "Wordy" for Most Ludicrous Combination of Antonyms in a Sentence goes to . . .*

In showbiz, you can make it big, but you can't make a living. Everyone knows you do whatever it takes, and cheating is probably the least horrible of it all.

Just like in sports, the "powers that be" have an incentive to encourage slimy behavior. Whether it's getting quiz show answers in advance, backstabbing your cabana-mates on a desert island, or lip-synching the national anthem, cheating increases buzz and drama, which increases viewership, attendance, and merchandising, which makes studio execs, advertisers, ex-wives, and lawn boys very, very rich and very, very happy.

# Big Brother Isn't Watching You

If you cheat correctly in politics, you'll be in charge of the enforcement agencies, so *they* won't stop you. If they try to, just fire them, a la Alberto Gonzales and the Mystery of the Fired Prosecutors (which happens to be the title of the next Harry Potter book).

Not only that, but government bureaucrats surely won't rock the boat to tattle on their bosses, coworkers, employees, and fellow prostitute clientele.

# Taking Care of Business

*Whoa, Nellie.* Our legal system loves corporate cheaters and affords them privileges ordinary criminals can't imagine. Crime does pay, at least massive corporate crime, thanks to a systematic double standard. The savings and loan disaster of the 1980s cost taxpayers over $500 billion, but those involved got an average of only two years in jail. Compare that with the five-, ten-, and fifteen-year sentences doled out for petty crimes like robbery or drug trafficking. Crack cocaine carried ten times the mandatory sentence of powder cocaine because, obviously, crack is prevalent among the poor while powder coke is found among the wealthy (i.e., Great Cheaters).

> **In$piration:** *"Most if not all of those who commit white-collar crime are distinguished by lives of privi-*

*lege, much of it with origins in class inequality. . . .*
*When they confront officialdom or mid-level bureau-*
*crats, they receive polite and sympathetic hearing."** 

Rest assured, when it comes to penalties, we look more harshly on someone holding up a 7-Eleven or selling drugs than someone who cheats thousands of people out of their jobs, savings, and futures. Steal a slice of pizza three times? *Life in jail.* Send Flint, Michigan, back to the stone age? *A nice little severance package.*

Our system of financial regulation relies on hard-working, dedicated, well-funded regulators committed to bringing vague violations of loose rules to light. *Good luck with that.* The SEC (the Securities and Exchange Commission, a.k.a., Stealing Equals Cool) is supposed to protect investors—your main targets—but, really, it can't and it won't. It's underfunded, inexperienced, understaffed, and unable to meet even modest targets.

- In 1980, the SEC reviewed almost every company filing. By 2000, it was down to 8 percent. By 2010, you have to call the SEC yourself to report your crimes, then *maybe* they'll get to it after nap time.
- The staff is about the same size as it was in the 1940s, when 260 million shares traded on the NYSE each *year.* Now? About two billion are traded each *day.*

---

* Neal Shover and John Paul Wright, eds., *Crimes of Privilege* (New York: Oxford University Press, 2001).

- The SEC budget has been cut by 25 percent, even as corporate scandals increase. You can earn more during lunch than most investigators do all year. *Yum.*

Even the few avenues for cracking down on corporate crime are being closed off. SEC Chief Christopher Cox pushed regulations to protect executives, corporations, and accountants from fraud accusations, mostly because he's totally awesome. And the busting of such corporate pains-in-the-ass as Eliot Spitzer and Richard Scruggs will enable you to speed down the cheating highway without even turning on the radar detector: All the cops are in jail.

Business schools breed Great Cheaters left and right.* Most MBA programs don't even have ethics classes. If they do, there are no textbooks, just handouts, news clippings, hypotheticals, and lectures about how to avoid prosecution. Business school ethics simply teaches MBAs how not to get caught. They'll be your cheating peers or vice presidents soon.

"What about the Supreme Court? Won't they stop corporate crime?"

*Uh . . . no.* They've interpreted the Fourteenth Amendment—the one guaranteeing citizenship to recently freed slaves with the whole not depriving "any person of life, liberty, or property, without due process of law"—as a guarantee of

---

* A study by the Center for Academic Integrity at Duke University shows that 56 percent of MBA students admitted cheating, more than in any other U.S. graduate program.

rights to corporations as citizens. They've said money has the same protection as speech. Chief Justice John Roberts is such a business lover that the first dance at his wedding was just him, his wallet, and "Take the Money and Run." In recent years, he and his cohorts have wisely knocked down whistle-blower protections, approved massive pro-business tax breaks, severely limited the rights and abilities of shareholders and employees to pursue corporate malfeasance, stopped efforts to collect $280 billion from tobacco companies,* protected dangerous industries, and fed Walmart the souls of the small-business owner. The court realizes corporate leaders know what's best for the country and it should get out of their way so they can cheat America great.

As long as you're entertaining us, feeding us, and not interrupting our prime-time TV, we won't stop you. In fact, your cheating is becoming *more* accepted. Today's youth—tomorrow's employees, customers, and police—are bred to cheat: Parents force private preschools to enroll their children, then bribe doctors to diagnose learning disorders so the little darlings have more time on the SATs (even if their only learning disorder is "stupidity") and can go to colleges with ineffective "honor codes" and laughable grade inflation. These kids aren't interested in a "meaningful life." They just want

---

* In August 2006, a Federal court found the tobacco industry guilty of hiding health consequences, manipulating cigarette design to addict, and other forms of treachery but couldn't punish the companies because damages could not be imposed for past wrongs, only as remedies to restrain "future misdeeds." *Ha!* In the "future," we'll all be dead. *Thank you, wise men!*

money and are looking for shortcuts and easy scams along the way. They "get it" and so will you.

## End of the "Enron Era"

"But cheating is *soooooo* 2002." No, it's not.

Don't be discouraged by talk of "The End of the Enron Era." Yes, the dawn of the millennium has been an inspirational time for all cheaters. The Enron folks are in jail or worse, the real estate bubble burst, Marion Jones and Tim Donaghy have been busted, and even White Oprah had an ankle bracelet accessory . . . but the era of cheating isn't over.

*It never will be.*

> **In$piration:** "*The game never changes, just the players. The more there is to steal, the more it will be stolen . . .*" —John Jakobson, NYSE member since 1955*

Weren't the savings and loan scandals of the 1980s the end of corporate treachery? Weren't we supposed to have world peace after the fall of the USSR? Wasn't government corruption over with Watergate and Iran-Contra? Wasn't I supposed to have gotten taller after eighth grade?

*How's all that working out?*

There will always be opportunities to cheat. It's up to you to discover them, to create new ways to Get Rich Cheating. Seek out new unexplored worlds, boldly cheat where no

---

\* Eric Weiner, *What Goes Up* (New York: Little, Brown and Company, 2005).

cheater has cheated before. Be the next Barry Bonds, Ashlee Simpson, Rod Blagojevich, or generic, balding, middle-aged white corporate executive.

It's your patriotic duty to present new challenges to the authorities, to keep 'em sharp. Repeat techniques from the past to profit in the future. Institutional memory is short. Public memory is even shorter. By the time you read this, everyone will have forgotten what happened yesterday, and you can do it again. Someone once said, "Those who do not learn from history are bound to be duped by the Great Cheaters like you."

*I think that someone was me.*

## Reform

Every now and then, in every industry, the watchdogs promise to revamp their inadequate enforcement techniques. They pass new drug-testing rules, or toothless regulations like Sarbanes-Oxley,* or campaign finance laws, or lobbying regulations, or blah, blah, blah. These are tales full of sound and fury, signifying squadoosh.

The spring 2008 re-regulation of financial markets was really just rearranging the acronyms of various agencies to spell S.C.R.E.W. T.H.E. P.O.O.R. It was only an attempt to create the appearance of regulation. Same with all the post-collapse hand-wringing, bloviating, and harrumphing.

---

\* Signed in 2002, the Sarbanes-Oxley Act—also known as SarbOx, SOX, or Sucky McStupid Law—was the only attempt to address corporate crime of that era. It addressed corporate crime by saying, "Hello, Corporate Crime. Please be bothered with some technicalities, but otherwise go about your business."

Timid scamsters worry that a Democratic administration will clamp down on cheating industries . . . but it was Clinton who deregulated telecommunications and North American exploitation, er, trade, and Carter freed up airlines to fly the unregulated skies. The structural framework to Get Rich Cheating won't change significantly under Obama. Maybe you'll have to learn new code words or spend bribes to access the new power players or label some proposals "socialist" to defeat them. But talk of "reform" is just a lot of hot air and no action. Hot air alone won't stop your plans (unless you're trying to eliminate hot air, which, frankly, seems like a dumb plan).

Some whiners may still demand a new "ethics" on your part. There's a theory that says you've got "duties" as a member of society. Guess what? You have to balance your duties to *society* against your duty to *you*. When you die, who's gonna be there? Society? No, it's just going to be you and your greedy heirs. If you have enough money, your heirs will dance like monkeys to please you . . . so don't worry about "society."

At worst, new ethical rules or half-hearted regulations will force you to get creative about how you cheat, whom you cheat, and with what science and technology you cheat. Necessity is the mother of invention, greed is its father, and you will be their rich bastard son.

# 5

# Are You Ready for
# Some Cheating?

## Get Rich Cheating Pre-Screening

Before you move on to Part II, How to Cheat, ask yourself: Do you have what it takes to be a Great Cheater? This is important, so don't lie—at least not yet. *Get Rich Cheating* isn't for those who want to save a few bucks on their taxes. It's for people who want to use deceit, fraud, lies, and trickery to make millions and billions and *trillions* of dollars, i.e., Great Cheaters.

Can you be one of them?

## What You DON'T Need
    Intelligence
    Compassion
    Leadership ability
    Humility

Vision
Competence
A soul

## What You DO Need

A burning desire to have riches beyond reason
Undiagnosed psychoses
Megalomania
Willful disregard for the well-being of others
Mother issues
Father issues
Lack of morals
Sincere insincerity
A good poker face
A list of enemies, both real and imagined
Inability to feel remorse or shame
A belief that, since we're all finite beings, what we do with
 our lives has no bearing on the greater cosmic journey
 of the Universe

 Still not sure if you're cheating material? Then take this twenty-one-point Cheating Competence Test. Answer key follows.

  1. Are you turned on by the words "greed," "self-interest,"
   and "bastard?"
  2. When was your first shoplifting experience?

3. As a child, did you blame things on an imaginary friend? As an adult?

4. When's the last time you lied on your resume? Why have you waited so long?

5. Do you believe in an afterlife where all our sins are tabulated?

6. How often do you pretend to sleep in order to overhear conversations?

7. Do you have a place to stash your wedding ring on "business trips"?

8. Are you a psychopath? Really? Are you sure? C'mon, not even a little?

9. Which of the following would you do for a dollar: sell out your best friend, take steroids, get a sex change, or kill a hobo? What about $10?

10. When an old woman falls down, do you: laugh, offer to help but steal her wallet, sell her some worthless Florida real estate, or all of the above?

11. Do you cheat at racquetball, golf, and/or child-rearing?

12. If you were caught cheating, sent to jail, then wrote a best-selling tell-all book, would that be good enough for you?

13. Is "business ethics" an oxymoron? Is "ethics" even a word?

14. Do material possessions make up for physical short-comings? What is the accepted dollars-to-inch ratio?

15. Do you like to lie? Is it a thrill when you get away with it? Tell the truth. You love it, right? No? Yes? Wait, do you? What does "no" mean? Is "no" really "yes"?

16. Do you like cutting in line?

17. Food and sex: Do you think about anything else?

18. Punky Brewster or Alex P. Keaton?

19. Are you willing to create a public panic by fabricating a disease and/or plague for which only your company has the antidote? Even if it meant making billions and billions of dollars?

20. Is the public "stupid," "gullible," or "on the cutting edge of tomorrow's future?"

21. When you watch a horror film, to whom do you most relate? The terrorized but nubile teenagers, Freddy Krueger, studio executives, or the short brown women selling pirated copies in the subway?

## Answer Key

If you answered *any* of the above questions *in any way*, I'm sorry, but you're not ready to cheat. Please tell your parents that you're a failure.

If, however, you skipped ahead to this answer key without even reading the questions, congratulations! You're ready to Get Rich Cheating!

You may proceed.

# Part II

# How to Cheat

# 6

## Pick Your Poison

### Choose Your Cheat

You want to Get Rich Cheating. Great. But how exactly? No one ever made a fortune stealing office supplies, so think big. This is the hardest part. As many rappers have plagiarized, "Six million ways to die. Choose one."

Maybe there aren't *six million* ways to cheat, but if you want to Get Rich Cheating, there are four main professions from which to choose: sports, business, entertainment, and politics. When weighing the pros and cons, don't consider your talent but rather what you want, what you can tolerate, and how you can best Get Rich Cheating.

*"Is one industry better than the others?"*

Meh, I don't know.

*"Can I pick more than one?"*

Sure, why not. We need more girls who look like Dick Cheney and can dunk.

*"Should I do more than one?"*

# Get Rich Cheating

Do I look like your mother? Stop asking questions, pick a profession, and get rich already. Sheesh.

## INDUSTRY: SPORTS

EXAMPLES: Roger Clemens, Mark McGwire, Shawne Merriman, Floyd Landis, Ben Johnson, the 1919 White Sox, Pete Rose, the New York Yankees, Tim Donaghy, Clemson football

BENEFITS: Culture willing to shower you in coin, owners to profit from your freak physique, fans, joy of victory

DRAWBACKS: The inexorable march of time, better cheaters on other teams, shrunken testicles

CHICKS: Dig it

## INDUSTRY: BUSINESS

EXAMPLES: Enron's Ken Lay, ExxonMobil's Lee Raymond, Montgomery Burns of *The Simpsons*

BENEFITS: Appearance doesn't matter. You can get fat, grow old, and stay ugly.

DRAWBACKS: Unions, domestic help, humidity in the Hamptons, nagging suspicion that you *can't* take it with you, paperwork

CHICKS: Dig your money

## INDUSTRY: ENTERTAINMENT

EXAMPLES: Paris Hilton, Jay Mohr, Tori Spelling, Pam Anderson, Jayson Blair

BENEFITS:  Adoring fans
DRAWBACKS: Tabloids, drunk driving laws, love scenes
with Tom Cruise, adoring fans
CHICKS:    Oh, diggity dig dig. Hot, desperate, and
crazy.

## INDUSTRY: POLITICS

EXAMPLES:  George W. Bush, Rudy Giuliani, Jack
Abramoff, Chicago Mayor Richard J. Daley,
Tammany Hall
BENEFITS:  Money *and* power? Yes!
DRAWBACKS: Public scrutiny, "listening" to "the people,"
never again saying what you actually be-
lieve, voters
CHICKS:    Dig it, but might get you impeached

No matter which industry you choose—whether you sell
widgets,* hit baseballs, make bad movies, or run the Senate
Armed Services Committee—you must think of yourself as
the head of the organization called "You." You are CEO of
You Inc., running the business of You. All your decisions
from this point forward must be focused on *your* bottom
line and how to nudge it higher while everyone looks the
other way.

---

*  By "widget" I mean neither the Ewok nor the things on Mac computers, but rather
the common term for a hypothetical product. Duh.

# Enter at Your Own Rich

Once you've picked your cheating career, how do you enter your chosen cheating industry? Work hard, study, train, stay focused, make sacrifices . . . *Ah ha ha! Gotchya! Totally kidding.* Listen, there are simple ways to begin. Here are some favorites.

## Family Ties

Nepotism is defined by the CED* as "the easy way in." If you're lucky, you can use it like a Great Cheater:

- Be a famous person's offspring and become a famous person yourself. Tori Spelling has no discernible talent, but her dad made Hollywood "hits." George Clooney may be handsome, but he and his mullet got a head start because his aunt was Rosemary Clooney. Liza Minnelli became a sensation because Judy Garland was adorable . . . and her baby-momma-momma, i.e., her momma. *Who's your momma?*

- Many people voted for George W. Bush because they thought he was his father and that he'd return their waistlines to 1992 levels; the Romneys, Gores, Adamses, and Roosevelts had children who parlayed popularity into support; the Kennedy clan has endured shootings, plane crashes, convictions, and car accidents but keeps popping out senators, attorneys general,

---

* Cheaters English Dictionary.

pundits, and wives of Austrian-ish governors; and we'll only know how strong the Clinton line is at the end of Chelsea's second term.

- The list of those who hand corporate power over to children is infinite. If you're lucky, you can take over a family business. Your dad owns a paper company? Good for you! Confirm that you're in his will, buy some odorless poison, invite him over for a "drink," and let nature take its course. Welcome to CEO-ville. Population: You.

- Even in sports, where "athletic ability" should prevail, a name will get you scouted and earn you a few breaks. The Boones, Yannick Noah, and Peyton and Eli Manning all had championship-caliber last names. But why take the risk with a different *first* name? Just throw a junior on the end of Dale Earnhardt and Ken Griffey, and you're guaranteed a signing bonus. Or heck, have your dad call all his children "George Foreman"—even the girls.

## Buy Your Way In

Say your powerful family doesn't have influence in the industry you want to cheat—not everyone wants to be a perforated-notepad magnate, you know. It can still get you access to the reins of cheating. Ever see anyone fail out of, or not get into, an elite college when there's a building on campus with his last name? *Me neither.* Paris Hilton's the heiress to the Hilton hotels, which has *what* to do with being whatever it is that she is? *Nothing*. Money can't buy her love, but it can buy her people who make B-list movies and sex tapes, which is, in fact, a kind of "love."

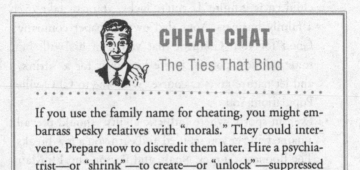

## CHEAT CHAT
### The Ties That Bind

If you use the family name for cheating, you might embarrass pesky relatives with "morals." They could intervene. Prepare now to discredit them later. Hire a psychiatrist—or "shrink"—to create—or "unlock"—suppressed memories of emotional, physical, and/or sexual abuse in your childhood—or "youth." Those jerks don't deserve a say in your life, especially after you make a weepy national television appearance disclosing their cruelty.

## The Casting Couch

Speaking of love, when it comes to *entering* an industry, or *rising* within it, remind those making decisions of the old proverb "I get in, you get in." It's the casting couch, pioneered by Great Cheater and studio director Darryl Zanuck.* Have you seen an action movie lately? You know the stars' real tal-

---

* Zanuck, one of the first big Hollywood studio heads, was actually born in Wahoo, Nebraska, a town probably next to the Municipality of Whoopee.

ent isn't "acting"—it's their bodies. The springs in the casting couch have squeaked from China to India, from boy bands* to B movies, from the ladies and the gents. So do it: Not only is it a path to riches, but if you close your eyes and pretend to be somewhere else, it can also be fun!

## Land the Job

As an aspiring corporate cheat, you can also be hired to run a company the old-fashioned way: Lie on your resume. A foundation of falsehoods early in your career makes it easier to maintain that deception as you cheat through the years.

The fake resume is, along with jazz and stand-up comedy, one of the great American art forms, loaded with inaccuracies ever since T. Rex claimed to type eighty words per minute and have "tar-pit immunity." You want to be CEO of Ford? Your resume should say you ran Toyota for ten years after graduating summa cum laude from Harvard, Princeton, and Yale with joint degrees in Auto Company Management and Making Detroit Great Again. (Sometimes a resume is called a "CV," shorthand for the Latin *curriculum vitae*, or the Olde English *cheat verily*.)

*Be careful.* Only lie about things that are relevant to the job into which you're weaseling. George O'Leary claimed he had a master's degree when applying to coach football at

---

* Lou Pearlman, the creator of the Backstreet Boys, 'NSync, and many other 1990s boy bands, seduced one member of each group as the price for their fame.

Notre Dame. *You don't need to know Descartes to draw up a blitz package.* David Edmondson of RadioShack lied about attending Bible College. *Bible College?* That's like lying about going to summer camp. No one cares if you can whittle or know how many commandments there are—*hint: more than seven*—they just want to know if you can pretend to do the job. If you absolutely must lie recklessly—and I respect that—at least do it about something cool, like attributing your weight loss to eating Subway when it was clearly stomach surgery. (I'm looking at you, Jared.)

Once you've lined up all your impressive credentials, prep the two, and only two, Great Cheater interview skills: bribery and physical threats. Note:

- Always introduce a bribe with the phrase "in theory." For instance, "In theory, if I were to give you a brief-case full of Pakistani currency, could we move this whole thing along?"
- When making threats, be sure to mention the family members of your interviewer by name. Shows you're serious *and* detail-oriented.

You'll receive a job offer in a few days.

## Start Your Own Company

What if you don't want to go through the lengthy job search? Maybe you don't like breaking into established hierarchies, you hate interviews, you don't like people, or you're illiterate.

*Pleez d-oo n-ah-t wuhr-ee.* I'm not here to judge you. I'm here to help you blackmail the judge who'll judge you, but that's covered in Part III.

So, start your own company. It's easy! Just fill out some paperwork, and—*pow!*—you're running your very own WorldCom Junior.

A few notes about starting a company:

1. *Company name.* This is the first impression you make, your initial chance to fool customers, investors, fans, and the government. Choose a name people can trust, even if it's for a company they can't. Consider warm, inviting words like "love," "safe," "chocolate," and "freedom." Don't include suspicion-raising phrases like "lie," "cheat," "steal," "bait 'n' switch," or "I swear I never touched her, Officer."

   Still not clear? Take this test. Which is better: "U.S. Savings & Loan" or "My Place 2 Steal Ur Ca$h"?

2. *Mission possible.* You'll need a Mission Statement. It outlines the philosophies and goals that guide your company. You cannot tell the truth here. Allude to vague notions of saving the world and deliver a message that says, in essence, "Whoever you are, this company will make you richer, thinner, and younger. And taller, if that's your thing. Heck, you want a new hairstyle? We can do that, too. Just give us some money. God Bless America."

3. *Prophylactic measures.* Include an indemnification clause to make sure that you are protected against, and reimbursed for, any "mistakes" or "errors." Not that anything would go wrong on *your* watch, but, you know, just in case, say, $10 million goes missing. All the cool CEOs do it.*

4. *Attention to detail.* When filling out any legal forms, make lots of typos, use a very small font, cross-reference nonexistent third-party documents,** and toss in phrases like "n/a," "information available upon request," "whatever," and "whatchyoutalkin' 'bout, Willis?" as often as possible.

5. *Organizational structure.* In order to make clear how your company will operate, make an organizational chart. The public one should look like the top one, opposite. The real one, posted everywhere your employees might see, has the structure shown in the bottom illustration.

---

\* Like Caremark Rx's Edwin Crawford. He's the dreamiest . . . and Get Rich Cheatingest.
\*\* See Attached Addendum Part XLXI, Subsection 2(a)ii, Paragraph Fliggedydorp.

## Pick Your Poison

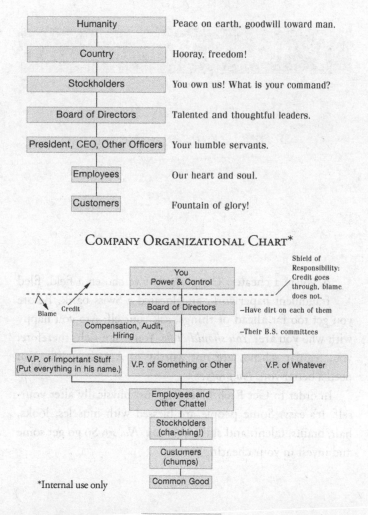

### THE HUMBLE & RESPECTFUL COMPANY
### ORGANIZATIONAL CHART

| | |
|---|---|
| Humanity | Peace on earth, goodwill toward man. |
| Country | Hooray, freedom! |
| Stockholders | You own us! What is your command? |
| Board of Directors | Talented and thoughtful leaders. |
| President, CEO, Other Officers | Your humble servants. |
| Employees | Our heart and soul. |
| Customers | Fountain of glory! |

### COMPANY ORGANIZATIONAL CHART*

You
Power & Control

Shield of Responsibility: Credit goes through, blame does not.

Blame     Credit

Board of Directors —Have dirt on each of them

Compensation, Audit, Hiring —Their B.S. committees

V.P. of Important Stuff (Put everything in his name.)     V.P. of Something or Other     V.P. of Whatever

Employees and Other Chattel

Stockholders (cha-ching!)

Customers (chumps)

Common Good

*Internal use only

# 7

## Make Yourself Great

*We can rebuild him . . .*
*Better, stronger, faster . . .*
—*THE SIX MILLION DOLLAR MAN*

*. . . richer*
—YOU

So, you're a cheater. Congrats. You've chosen a field, filed fraudulent paperwork, and located a Swiss bank. Before you get too far ahead of things, ask yourself: Are you happy with who you are? *You shouldn't be.* You're not rich; therefore, you, regular schmo, are not worthy of American life. You need a better you. *No problem.*

In order to Get Rich Cheating, just physically alter yourself. It's easy. Some people are blessed with muscles, looks, hair, brains, talent, and skills. *Not you. No, sir.* So go get some and invest in your cheating future.

## Plastic Surgery

In these days of superficial self-worth, young girls get breast implants for their sweet sixteen birthdays, thirty-year-olds inject botulism into their brows to attain a couple hours of expressionless beauty, and Lord knows what the hell happened to Michael Jackson's face . . . *but he's still making money, isn't he?*

Plastic surgery is the gift that Great Cheaters give themselves, especially in the entertainment industry, where looks are everything. No one *really* gets tight abs on eight minutes a day. It takes at least a two-hour procedure to suck all the fat from your body and eventually replace it with thousand-dollar bills. You think Pamela Anderson would be famous if she wasn't an impossibly plastic Barbie doll? No. Once *you* can bounce quarters off every part of your body, you'll never need such small change again.

Ever been to the Playboy Mansion? Of course not. You wouldn't be at home reading this on a Saturday night if you had. Well, let me tell ya, Hef's house is filled with high-pitched arguments between the pre- and post-implant generations about which models are more legit and which are cheaters. No one, however, argues over which make better flotation devices.

There were about twelve million cosmetic plastic surgeries in the U.S. in 2007.* Women got bigger breasts, plumper

---

* Miranda Hitti, "More Going Under the Knife to Look Sharp," WebMD. http://www.webmd.com/skin-beauty/news/20080326/more-going-under-the-knife-to-look-sharp.

lips, tighter tummies, lifted lids, reshaped noses, and just a bit off the back. The fellas got *smaller* breasts, some fat moved around, a little "male enhancement," and hair restoration. Very few people added a third arm—you know, to steal wallets—but that might be too forward-thinking for this day and age. Give it five years.

Even if you're not in showbiz, a hot body will help you earn a bigger cheat-check. You can climb the corporate ladder more quickly if those above you get a nice cleavage shot when looking down; millionaire athletes like cheerleaders just as much as the rest of us; and with a smooth, young, gender-neutral physique, you're guaranteed the spot as a congressman's top aide. *E pluribus unum, indeed.*

Don't be limited to superficial surgery either. Functional changes under the knife can have an economic impact too. Bernie Williams is among a handful of pro athletes who've gotten laser eye surgery. After he did it, he hit .342, the highest in his career. Guess what? It was also a contract year. *Cha-cha-cha-ching.*

*Are there drawbacks to plastic surgery?* Well, if one thing about you is obviously fake, people—including yourself—may wonder what else is fake, think you're hiding behind a mask you can never remove, and start calling you an exotic dancer with father issues. These people—including yourself—are jealous, ignorant, and poor. Ignore their questions and go buy some new lips that can tell 'em to buzz off.

## Stylists

If you don't have the stomach for surgery, or you realize the knife can only improve so much (hello again, Tori Spelling!), hire a stylist to cheat your appearance.* Ever notice the change from the preliminary rounds of *American Idol* to the finals? It's not more talent, it's more hair gel and black clothing. Who did that? *Stylists.* They'll get you nicer clothes, help you lose weight, remove your eyebrows, and provide the latest hip accessory, be it a Chihuahua or an African baby. (Don't worry—if you get tired of either, you can throw 'em away.)

Invest a little in someone to re-create you. Ambush makeovers like *The Swan* and *Queer Eye for the Poor Guy.* Isn't that cheating? Covering up who you really are, pretending to be something else, all in order to impress, seduce, or fool others into loving, respecting, and, eventually, paying you more? Yes, it is. So don't go it alone. You obviously have no sense of fashion, or you wouldn't be reading this. Your assistant would be.

## Buy Another You

Pay someone to do the work for you. *Wanna be a famous singer?* You don't need to sing. Milli Vanilli and Ashlee Simpson are well-paid celebutards who've lip-synched their way to fame and fortune. Heck, the glorified karaoke contest *American Idol* encourages contestants to avoid originality at all costs.

---

* Don't forget do-it-yourself plastic surgery techniques like anorexia and bulimia! You don't need a stomach for them.

Miley Cyrus has used body doubles, and Lipitor used one for spokesman Dr. Robert Jarvik.*

# Performance-Enhancing Drugs

Performance-enhancing drugs. PEDs. Probably what you thought this whole book was about.

The purpose of medicine—*the reason for science*—is not to heal the sick: they're worthless lost causes. Humans pursue progress in order to turn ordinary men into gods, to help an aspiring crook like you become a Great Cheater. This is your time: Open the sports page of today's paper, and you'll see examples for you, your children, and your children's mutant children's children.

Here are some FAQs about PEDs for those of you looking to build big enough muscles to carry all the gold you can cheat.

### *What are performance-enhancing drugs?*

Generally, they are hormone treatments that increase the buildup of cell tissues, particularly muscles. *And the choices!* You've got anabolic steroids like tetrahydrogestrinone (THG), human growth hormone (HGH), testosterone (for the ladies!), amphetamines, strychnine, androstenedione, erythropoietin (EPO), blood doping, and even brandy. They help you heal from injuries, have greater endurance, thinner blood,

---

\* The company claimed it was the sixty-year-old doctor sexily rowing a manly-man boat across Lake Pants-on-Fire in a popular ad. It wasn't.

more oxygen, make you look younger and healthier, and get you stronger, faster, and drunker.

### Who uses them?

Everyone and everything, from humans to horses to Ahnold. The known PED *scandals* (i.e., careless cheaters who got caught) include athletes from football, soccer, baseball, shot put, skiing, sprinting, marathoning, and cycling. Table tennis has yet to be hit by a steroid scandal, but it will. I guarantee it.*

A few names: Barry Bonds, Floyd Landis, Ben Johnson, Marion Jones, Mark McGwire, Shawne Merriman, Roger Clemens, the *horses* from several 2008 Olympic equestrian teams, and most of 1950–1990 Germany east of the Berlin Wall. They broke records, won races, got medals, grew man-boobs, became champions, movie stars, governors, and harbingers of the Apocalypse . . . and that's just Ahnold.

Athletes are the best-known beneficiaries of PEDs, but it's not just them. Academic researchers have admitted using stimulants like Adderall and Provigil to maintain focus and work faster and more efficiently. What about Viagra and Propecia and Zoloft? They make you perform better. PEDs have even been linked to—but "denied" by—entertainers like Mary J. Blige (a lady!), Sylvester Stallone, Wyclef Jean, and 50 Cent, who came close to stealing the idea for this book with his album *Get Rich or Die Trying*. To misquote Yoda, "There is no try, Mr. 50; there is only Get Rich Cheating."

---

* Not a guarantee.

# Get Rich Cheating

### *How many athletes use PEDs?*

In baseball alone: lots. As chronicled by the annoying and ultimately ineffective Mitchell Report,* Major League Baseball has a particularly glorious record of steroid and HGH use. Estimates vary from the eighty-nine names listed in the report, to David Wells's speculation that 40 percent of players are using, to Jose Canseco's much higher guess of 85 percent, to Mark McGwire's "Arrgh, Thag smash ball!" Extrapolating from the Mitchell Report, by 2012, not only will every player be on performance enhancers, but two out of every five fans will be required to juice just to enter the park.

### *Why do athletes use PEDs?*

First, to become a professional athlete. You gotta break into the pros before you can cheat a ridiculous salary.

Second, once you're in, you can boost your performance to score a huge payday leap into the pantheon of Great Cheaters. A big year means a big contact. A bad year means playing in the minors, or worse: Kansas City. Ken Caminiti, the 1996 National League MVP said after juicing up a .326 average, 40 HRs, and 130 RBIs, "Look at all the money in the game: You have a chance to set your family up, to get your daughter into a better school . . . I can't say, 'Don't do it,' when the guy next to you is as big as a house and he's going to take your job and make the money."** Yes, your daughter might have webbed feet

---

\* Baseball Commissioner Bud Selig had former Senator George Mitchell conduct an investigation into anabolic steroids and HGH use. His four-hundred-plus-page 2007 report named eighty-nine players who allegedly used enhancers. *What a little narc jerk.*
\*\* David Callahan, *The Cheating Culture*, p. 75.

and there's a good chance you'll break her arm in a fit of rage, but at least she'll get into Wesleyan.

Third, to win. Vince Lombardi famously said, "Winning isn't everything, it's the only thing." What are the less famous words that came next? "Now stick this syringe where the sun don't shine." In a 1995 survey of nearly two hundred athletes, more than half said they'd take a drug to help win every competition for five years, even if they knew it'd kill them after that period.* That was fourteen years ago, before PEDs became cool—basic extrapolation suggests that 317 percent of athletes would say so now.

### *Why don't more people use PEDs?*

Well, in addition to the needle prickings, you've gotta pay for masking agents and chemists and doctors to make sure it's done right. The authorities are pretending to investigate, so you have to hide it, and, like Vikings running back Onterrio Smith, may even need the embarrassingly floppy Original Whizzinator. You must monitor your drug intake so your head doesn't explode before you cash out, but if East Germany could do it, so can you. Heck, East Germany isn't even around anymore. But you are, aren't you? Sitting around, all flabby, slow, and poor, just dreaming about getting rich. You want to be rich, right? What's a little extra effort? Get up off your fat ass and plunge a needle into it!

---

* Callahan, p. 76.

# Get Rich Cheating

***I've heard people say they're bad. Well?***

The pursuit of Great Cheaters using PEDs has become a witch hunt, and everyone with a newspaper column, blog, or receding hairline is an angry villager with a torch. *Who are all these people to judge?* Think about the performance enhancers *they* take to get through life: caffeine, so they can work hard all day; nicotine, so when they realize they're getting screwed they can take a cigarette break; and alcohol, so they can get drunk each night, forgot about everything, and do it all again the next day! And why isolate only HGH and steroids as PEDs? Isn't cocaine a performance-enhancing drug for investment bankers, opium for writers, heroin for Scottish rock stars, marijuana for art history majors, crystal meth for crystal meth users, roofies for frat boys, alcohol for abusive husbands, and Old Spice for senators?

Sure, performance-enhancing drugs are not for everyone. Some ladies don't want a deep voice and moustache, and the fellas might not like acne and rage. But how do you know until you've tried it?

The point is, you need to put as much junk as possible in your body in order to succeed in your field and then cash in and get rich. You—as made by the Creator—are not good enough to do this on your own. Only after some surgery, fittings, body doubles, and injections will you be ready to Get Rich Cheating. Once all that's taken care of you can waive your option clause at the start of the season, hit .351 with fifty home runs, go on five 'roid rages, and get signed by the Yankees in December.

# 8

## Your Cheatin' Heart

*No one ever went broke underestimating*
*the intelligence of the American public.*
—H. L. MENCKEN

Cheating might not come naturally, but you need to get your head on straight if the rest of you is going to get on being crooked. To that end, here are some guiding principles for dealing with the outside world. The Great Cheaters live by them, so you should too. Repeat them to yourself every day, and they will carry you to riches.

### Your Cheating Philosophy

You must become a Great Cheater in your mind before you can become one in your life. Imagine yourself one, think like one, act like one, and live like one. Then you'll have no choice but to Get Rich Cheating: The bills alone will force you into it. A big part of your transformation is adopting a personal philosophy. It's not just about being immoral and unethical;

you need a clear-cut set of beliefs by which to live and rules to govern your every action.

## People Are Dumb

Everyone but you is a moron. Have you looked at our public school system? *Yuck.* Those are the "people" I'm talking about. They're your customers, employees, peers, and competition, your fans, audience, and constituencies, your investigators, prosecutors, and judges. They'll fall for your tricks, buy whatever you're selling, and be distracted by your shiny objects and clever lies.

## People Are Lazy Too

Much of Enron's improper behavior actually appeared in black and white in its corporate filings, but investors never took the time to read through it all. Dumb *and* lazy? *Excellent.*

## Exude Confidence

Even when you don't know what you're doing. Someone will believe you.

## Use Secrecy and Obfuscation

Language should be a barrier to understanding. You can't just say, "This transaction is designed to circumvent regulation 10(b)vii." Use small print, made-up words, nonsense. Everywhere. Be Dick Cheney. Use terms and phrases that project an air of authority but really mean nothing. "Global integration," "competitive balance," and "creative accounting" are just a few of the make-believe phrases that have gotten cheaters rich. *Superfantastical!*

## Obey the Letter, Not the Spirit, of the Law

Rules were made to be broken, loopholes were made to be exploited, you were made to be rich.

## Spin, Baby, Spin

You can make anything mean anything. Turn billions in "losses" into billions in "opportunities." Truth is just an obstacle to your reality. Learn to rationalize everything.

## There Are So Many Cheaters, They Can't Catch Us All

Can they?

## I Didn't Do It

And if I did, it wasn't my fault.

## I've Got Nothing to Hide

But please don't look in there.

**CHEAT CHAT**

Google's motto is "Don't Be Evil," which explains why they're just a tiny little company that will never make any real money, doesn't it?

## Cheating Character Traits

While the above principles inform your dealings with the outside world, your *virtues* are your internal road map. You will be alone for much of the Get Rich Cheating journey, and these will guide you. You need your moral compass to point due north, toward the Arctic Circle, where you will use the drill bit of cheating to bore beneath the ice of self-doubt to plunder the Russian oil reserves of wealth.

You are a sociopath alpha male whose desire to be loved is trumped only by his need to crush those who would love him. You are awkward around women and other humans. (Don't worry, you'll soon be rich enough for the best prostitutes and sexual harassment settlements money can buy.)

Values, integrity, conscience? I'm sorry, you wanted to read *Get Rich Never*. This is the real world, this is *Get Rich Cheating*. Here are your new virtues.

## Arrogance

You are the greatest thing since sliced bread. You will dominate, crush, destroy, stab, and kill your competition because you are just so damn good. You can't succeed with timidity and quiet confidence. If it didn't work for the Jedi, it won't work for you.*

Ask any casual sports fan to describe Bill Belichick, coach of the New England Patriots. What are the first words they'll use? Arrogant. Bastard. Jerk. Well, he is. He's short with reporters, doesn't answer questions, and clearly thinks anyone who's not him isn't worthy of his time and can't possibly comprehend his awesomeness.

What are the ninth or tenth words they'll use? Winner. Champion. He's won three Super Bowls, led his team to the only 16–0 regular season in history, and is pretty much acknowledged as one of the greatest coaches of all time. Thanks to all that, he's rich too. So rich that a $500,000 fine for spying on opposing teams barely dented his pocketbook.

(The eleventh or twelfth word? Cheater. So what? No one goes to eleven.)

On the other hand, look at Jerome Kerviel, the mundane, mild-mannered trader at Société Générale in France. What was he? Bland. What did he do? He lost $7.2 billion of his company's money in fraudulent trades. What else did he do? He got caught and didn't get rich. According to those

---

* Yes, it turned out okay in the end, but no one wants the modern equivalent of Jar Jar Binks.

who knew him, Kerviel just wanted some respect and a good bonus; he blended in and didn't want to make waves. With such lame, provincial aspirations, is it any wonder he failed?

Politicians are the kings, queens, and ombudsmen of arrogance and entitlement. The obnoxious prickishness of Eliot Spitzer, Dick Cheney, Sarah Palin, and the like is the reason God invented the punch to the face. Even after he was arrested and told not to, Governor Blagojevich and his hair appointed Roland Burris to the Senate. Our former Commander-in-Cheat George W. Bush issued over 150 signing statements, which basically said that more than 1,100 provisions of federal law—including rules about the military, immigration, affirmative action, whistleblowers, scientific research, and proper grammar—do not apply to him. Why? Because he wanted to and because he can. Why else? Because he's rich and powerful and lounging around in some country without an extradition treaty. Aren't you entitled to some cheating too?

Businessman Conrad Black led a lavish, extravagant, unnecessarily showboating life and made millions cheating. The CEOs of the "Big Three" automakers heroically flew expensive private jets to ask Congress for $25 billion because they were "broke."* Roger Clemens got a U.S. congressman to call him "a great American." Steven Schwarzman, head of Blackstone Private Equity, has become "the designated villain of an era on Wall Street."** Yeah, so? He also was able to throw himself

---

* Had they instead carpooled in one of their own vehicles, they would've been "broken down."
** James B. Stewart, "The Birthday Party," *The New Yorker*, February 11, 2008.

a $5 million sixtieth birthday party with Rod Stewart providing post-kitsch, irony-free nostalgic ambiance. Arrogance and self-indulgence are two sides of a very rich coin.

Be obnoxious. Black's a blowhard; Trump's a jerk; Tel-Save CEO Daniel Borislow told shareholders, "Shove it up your ass . . . You are not worthy of being in business, maybe life";* Enron's Jeff Skilling was known to bark at investors and reporters on conference calls; and Countrywide's Angelo Mozilo called an investor disgusting and unbelievable.** Not only does being a jerk get you "respect," it also might intimidate those who would investigate.

## Vengeance

The Great Cheater is vindictive, because when he's right, he lets everyone know. The former mayor of New York, Great Cheater Rudy Giuliani, created a "culture of retaliation"† that did what? *Got things done.* And what did that allow him to do? *Make millions after he left office.* He forced people to muzzle their opinions, had police officers, child care workers, and regular citizens arrested or fired if they disagreed with him or reported abuse, failings, or shortcomings. The city spent

---

* Alex Berenson, *The Number: How the Drive for Quarterly Earnings Corrupted Wall Street and Corporate America* (New York: Random House, 2003), p. 135.
** E. Scott Reckard, "Countrywide Financial Chairman Angelo Mozilo's E-mail Sets Off a Furor," *The Los Angeles Times*, May 21, 2008. He meant to forward the e-mail, not reply, but Great Cheaters don't have time for looking at where they're clicking. They've got poor people to scam.
† Michael Powell and Russ Buettner, "In Matters Big and Small, Crossing Giuliani Had Price," *The New York Times*, January 22, 2008.

$7 million settling civil rights suits and paying retaliatory damages from the Giuliani years. Seven million dollars. Guess who didn't pay a penny of that. *Rudy*. Guess who makes about that much each night on the speaker circuit. *Rudy*.

## Maintenance

If you stole a giant bag of Halloween candy, would you share it or obey some rule to eat only three pieces a day? No, you wouldn't. You'd hide it from your little sister and you'd eat and eat and eat until you got sick inside the bag; then you'd wash it off and eat some more. That's what happens when Great Cheaters are asked to give up power. They don't want to do it. They can't do it. Neither should you. Once you've got cheating power, money, status, and success, fight as long and as hard as you can to keep them, by any means necessary:

- Vladimir Putin named his aide Dmitry Medvedev to be his successor as Russian president. A few days later, Medvedev said he wanted Putin to be his prime minister. *How convenient*. Then Putin decided to broaden the prime minister's powers to pretty much that of, um, president.
- Al Davis, owner of the Oakland Raiders, is 357 years old.
- Franklin Roosevelt just couldn't let go of the presidency, so they passed the old Twenty-second Amendment.

- Having a spouse or child assume your position is kinda the same as keeping it yourself. You might not be the front man, but you keep the influence and power, and really, joint bank accounts are joint bank accounts, right Misters Clinton, Bush, Kennedy, Gore, and Steinbrenner? (I can't wait for the 2024 Jenna Bush presidential campaign).

- Athletes often use PEDs to extend their playing time. If not for recent revelations, Barry Bonds and Roger Clemens would have stayed in baseball until their heads got too large for their necks to support or the needle marks on their asses became visible from space. Would you rather have pure dominance for just a few years—like Pedro Martinez or Sandy Koufax—or reap the cash benefits over decades of pumped-up awesomeness? You can pay to change the record books later.

- Rudy Giuliani—former New York City mayor, unsuccessful Senate candidate, press-conference-informer-of-wife about plans to divorce—tried to change the rules of succession so that if he won a Senate seat, the mayoralty wouldn't go to Public Advocate Mark Green. He spent millions of taxpayer dollars on commissions to that effect. Since he didn't win, he was still mayor two years later when he used the tragedy of 9/11 to try to declare a city-wide state of emergency that would allow him to stay in office despite term limits. This would've made other famous Rudys—Huxtable and Ruttiger (of the movie *Rudy*)—very proud. They never gave up—why should he?

- Not to be outdone, Michael Bloomberg, Rudy's successor, wanted a third term because of the economic crisis, so he got the term limit rule changed. Must be something in the Lower Manhattan sewers that makes mayors greedy. Cheating alligators, perhaps?

## Evil-ance

Yes, young cheater, you can make tons of money cheating, but if you really, *really* want to be wealthy beyond all reason, as wealthy as the Great Cheaters, you must embrace what the unenlightened call "evil." When you Get Rich Cheating, evil is good. In order to fulfill their destiny, Great Cheaters must summon their inner demons. When *your* manifestation of darkness appears, he'll make you rich. He'll slither, hiss, smell like sulfur, and drool blood. Children will wail, animals will cower, and adults will give you money. Lots and lots of money.

It's good to be the villain. The villain always has the biggest castles, the toughest henchmen, the coolest gadgets, and the hottest babes. If you focus your energies, you can have them too.

This book provides just a taste of the many manifestations of evil. There's an infinite supply out there. Like the Great Cheaters, you must embrace the darkness that the weak—and the poor—shun. Don't worry about being able to look yourself in the mirror. You don't *need* to look yourself in the mirror: Mirrors only exist to confirm that you're the fairest of them all.

**Le$$on:** *Never make eye contact with yourself.*

## Cheating Cheaters' Cheat Sheet

Let's face it: Some people just don't "get it." They think it's "wrong" to Get Rich Cheating. This section is for dealing with them. Put a little yellow sticky on this page of talking points. These are the excuses to use on the unwashed mouth-breathers who vainly question your actions. Just remember, no matter what happens, when you're done arguing, you can always buy yourself happy.

- Everyone's cheating, especially your rivals. You're just "playing by the rules of a corrupt game."* You can't compete when everyone else is cheating. On the economic battlefield, you can't unilaterally disarm. (War imagery is *always* a winner.)
- As you gain wealth, it will benefit all of society and stimulate other sectors of the economy. You'll buy more houses and planes and companies, giving work to more nannies, chauffeurs, gardeners, and call girls. It's called trickle-down-into-your-wallet economics.
- Honesty and transparency are *not* good for the country. Sharing secrets weakens our positions.

---

* David Callahan, *The Cheating Culture.*

- Cheating provides practice for enforcement agencies. Keeps 'em sharp, helps 'em stay in shape. Great Cheaters are the training partners of the FBI.
- There has always been greed. It helps us evolve. I'm pretty sure someone in the Bible said, "Being selfish is next to being God-ish."
- Gigantic salaries are the only way to win the global war for talent. (War imagery: *still* a winner.)
- "I'm not a role model," said both Nicole Richie and Kimbo Slice. Neither are you. Parents are role models, Superman's a role model. *You* hire models for role *play*. See the difference? *Feel* the difference?
- For the business cheat, remember that the principal purpose of a corporation is to maximize returns to owners, i.e., to make *money*. A corporation is a living being that must profit to survive. If you don't allow it to do so, it will die. What's less ethical—making a few million by cheating . . . or *murder*?
- "How long have you been a communist?"
- "Will you only be happy when the terrorists win?"

Get Rich Cheating is about attitude. It's like "The Secret," but more lucrative. You must *believe* you can cheat. You must *believe* it will make you rich. You must *believe* in yourself and the cheatability of others. You ready? Good. Now let's get out there and Get Rich Cheating.

# 9

## Fir$t Things Fir$t

### Rich Better Have My Money

Y ou've got the job, you've got the attitude, and thanks to surgery you've got the biceps and the boobs. Now it's time to get paid.

I know regular pay doesn't seem like a sexy, unethical issue, but trust me, it is. The Great Cheaters know that getting so much for doing so little is the basis of the Get Rich Cheating method. The scams and ruses we'll discuss later are the cherries on top, but regular, legitimate paydays are the vanilla ice cream foundation of your sundae of deception.

Determine your pay immediately, and not just so you know how big a Caribbean Island to buy. You need to establish a relationship with your board of directors, team owner, or studio executive. By "establish a relationship," I mean "establish dominance and control." If they can't say no to you on compensation, they won't interfere with strategy, steroids, binge drinking, and putting adult entertainment on the corporate Amex. Your negotiations should go like this: You give a number and they counter with, "Is that all, sir?"

## "Performance"-Based Pay

Enhance your earnings by getting paid for your enhanced performance. It's a simple premise: If you do well, you get paid well.

- Hit fifty home runs—*cha-ching!*
- Get selected MVP or Cy Young—*cha-ching!*
- Make the All-Star Team—*cha-cha-ching!*
- Sell a million books, records, or tickets—*chippity-cha-chippity-ching!*
- Break the home run record in Yankee Stadium—*you're a rich, unloved record holder!*
- Have your sitcom go into reruns, get a million visitors to your website, be reelected as county comptroller—*roll around in the currency and coked-up fashion icons of your choice.*

Then, of course, there's the renegotiation period, when the next contract is based upon your performance in the previous one. This is where we separate the cheating men from the cheating boys. Jason Giambi signed a seven-year, $120 million contract in 2001 because he'd bravely sacrificed his testicles for a few home runs in the years before. Even while still with the lowly Oakland A's, his salary jumped from $315,000 in

1998 to $2,103,333 in '99 because of his juiced performance. Tom Cruise's per-film paycheck keeps going up even though he keeps getting weirder and weirder; Rudy Giuliani probably makes even more as a speaker now that he's run a presidential campaign; and Rush Limbaugh got a $400 million radio deal because he's been such a successful blowhard.

Honestly, though, when it comes to performance-based pay, no one does it better than corporate America. Take a look at the "rewards" given to some Great *Corporate* Cheaters (you've heard of some of these folks, but note how even the everyday Joe Schmo CEOs are cheating it big).

| EXEC | COMPENSATION | PERFORMANCE |
|---|---|---|
| Dennis Kozlowski, Tyco | $467 million in salary, bonuses, and stocks | Shareholders lost $93 billion during his four-year reign; made un-fun toys. |
| Bernie Ebbers, WorldCom | About $44 million | Company defrauded everyone for about $57 jillion. |
| Richard Clark, Merck | $14.5 million in 2007, 80 percent more than in '06 | Company paid $4.85 billion to settle lawsuits over Vioxx, which killed zillions and ruined thousands of spell checks. |

# Get Rich Cheating

| EXEC | COMPENSATION | PERFORMANCE |
| --- | --- | --- |
| Lee Raymond, ExxonMobil | $168 million in his final year alone | He's destroying the universe with his mind. |
| Michael Eisner, Disney | $220 million severance package | Taken out in a dramatic corporate coup that inspired James B. Stewart's best-selling book *DisneyWar*. (Story never made into a movie because of graphic violence and cartoon nudity.) |
| Franklin Raines, Fannie Mae | $148 million severance | The SEC said more than three years of misstated earnings would cause a multibillion-dollar restatement and wipe out profit. |
| Robert Nardelli, Home Depot | $210 million severance | Company lost $50 per share in value. |

| EXEC | COMPENSATION | PERFORMANCE |
| --- | --- | --- |
| Hank McKinnell, Pfizer | $213 million severance (including $305,000 to cover *unused vacation days*) | Company lost $137 billion in market value during his six years. |
| Dick Grasso, the New York Stock Exchange | $140 million severance | At the time, the NYSE was a *non-profit* organization. Obviously, he was selflessly taking all the profit to ensure the organization stayed true to its roots. |
| Tom Freston, Viacom | $50 million | Oversaw creation of *My Super Sweet 16.* |
| Richard Fuld, Lehman Brothers | Nearly $500 million from 1993–2007 | Ruined a perfectly nice 158-year-old Wall Street institution, jump-started the '08 financial crisis. |

Notice anything? *They made money, even though they did poorly.* A 2006 Corporate Library study showed eleven companies that lost $640 billion in shareholder value paid their CEOs $865 million, while ten companies who gained $82 billion in value paid only $190 million. In 2007, Wall Street's top banks gave management $39 billion in bonuses, and their companies only made $11 billion in profits!* That's a wordy, number-filled way of saying in corporate America, you'll get yours, whether you deserve it or not.

Notice something else? They made almost as much getting *fired* from their jobs as they did *doing* their jobs. Isn't that fantastic? They got paid to stink, and you should too. When you become a corporate CEO and you do things right—and by "right" I mean "running the company into the ground"—you're going to get fired. Isn't that a really, really, really, *really* good thing?** Sometimes these severance packages are called "golden parachutes" because you jump from the powerless airplane of your company and gently float onto a pile of gold money.

In this regard, it isn't just business cheaters who win by losing. Cheaters in all fields are routinely "bought out" by their employers, much to their financial gain. Indiana basketball coach Kelvin Sampson was accused by the NCAA of recruiting violations, was forced by the university to resign,

---

* Gregg Easterbrook, "The All-Unwanted All-Pros, conference championship analysis, and more," ESPN.com. http://sports.espn.go.com/espn/page2/story?page=easterbrook/080122&sportCat=nfl.

** The *New York Times* (liberal media!) studied the severance pay of workers and executives in terms of weeks of salary for each year of service. The average worker gets the equivalent of 2 weeks' pay for every year he or she worked at a company. The average CEO *without* a severance package gets 18 weeks per year worked. Great Cheaters with severance packages? McKinnell got the equivalent of 166 weeks, Eisner 536, Nardelli 568, and Disney's Michael Ovitz 5,034 weeks. That's 5,034 weeks of pay, per year worked. *It's good to be the cheat.*

and got a nice fat check for $750,000. Medical device maker Zimmer paid $250 million in buyouts to doctors to get out from under its trouble; Don Imus got millions to be fired for making racist remarks; and everyone from reporters to autoworkers are getting huge buyout offers just because they're part of obsolete business models. Failure pays!

Simply put, your goal should be to perform poorly enough to get a really bitchin' severance package. If your poor performance just so happens to earn you extra millions along the way, well, you might yet become a Great Cheater.

**Succes$tory:** *Hewlett-Packard's Carly Fiorina got paid $42 million when she was fired . . . and she's a girl!*

## CHEAT CHAT
### Justify Your Love

It's easy to explain why you deserve giant paychecks regardless of your performance. If the company makes billions: "I'm not *managing* the company; I took the risks to make it succeed. I'm an entrepreneur and should be paid like one." *Heads, you win.* If your company tanks: "Come on, I'm just *managing* this company, I shouldn't be treated as a risk-taking entrepreneur." *Tails, you win.*

## Options: Calendars Are for Wimps

Corporate America has another unique method for letting "performance" cheat you rich, both legitimately and "not so much": *stock options*. Options have been the driving force behind accounting scandals and corporate crime for years. You'd better learn to drive this force if you want to travel the Get Rich Cheating highway. *Don't worry: it's an automatic.*

Supporters of options say they align the interests of CEOs to those of their companies. Opponents claim CEOs pursue short-term gains for personal profit to the detriment of the long-term health of the company. You say, "I don't care; give me money."

Since the Feds are catching on, Great Cheaters have pioneered *backdating options*, a.k.a. time travel. Use 20/20 hindsight to change the date of the grant of the option to when the stock price was lowest: It'll seem like you bought when it was cheap, and you can sell whenever you want.* *Backdate.* Everyone's doing it. As of this writing, more than 37 kajillion companies were under investigation or conducting internal reviews. A University of Michigan study suggests that the options scandal may cost shareholders as much as $500 million, all so execs could get an average of $600,000 more per year. That's a great money-in-your-pocket to suffering-of-others

---

\* Lemme 'splain: Options give the holder the right to trade stock at a certain price at a certain time. When the holder exercises his options, he pays the price set on the date of the option grant and sells it at the sale price. If I'd been given options for 100 shares of GizmoCo stock when the price was $1 per share and I exercise those options when the price is $3 per share, I'll make ($3 per share [sale price] minus $1 per share [purchase price] times 100 shares = ) $200. I'm rich! *Thus endeth the math.*

ratio. Due to the scandal, CEOs like William McGuire of UnitedHealth Group have resigned, others have fled the country, and still others remembered they left the stove on and we haven't seen them since.

> **In$piration:** *McGuire was succeeded by Stephen Hemsley, who used to work at Arthur Andersen. Gee, I wonder where he learned his accounting tricks? Former employees shouldn't even include Arthur Andersen on their resumes anymore. It would raise fewer red flags if they wrote, "1997–2001: The Heroin Incident."*

Why is backdating options such a wonderful way to Get Rich Cheating?

- Backdating options isn't necessarily illegal; it just raises a bunch of accounting, tax, and disclosure issues. *Boooooring!*
- You don't need outsiders to look at a calendar, so it's easier to get things done, and there are fewer bodies to bury.
- It's not going to stop. An oversight board told Congress that the best way to resolve options backdating was, basically, to "stay out of the way" and let businesses reform themselves. Fox, meet Henhouse. Henhouse, Fox.
- It's nuanced, tricky, hard to follow. The man on the street won't care . . . unless your travels into the past

put him in touch with his birth parents and alter his future, which is really the present, thus jeopardizing his very existence . . . and to save his family, he'll need a professor named Doc, a flux capacitor, a DeLorean, and 1.21 gigawats!

**Succes\$tory:** *"Yeah, of course we ran a six-year backdating racket. Come on, we created Grand Theft Auto, and, heck, look at our name. We're telling everyone right there what we're up to."*

—Take-Two Interactive

If you're wary of this whole time travel thing, stick with basic option scams: Just before your options can be exercised, announce something big to boost the stock price in the short run. Whether it's true or not. Why do you think Steve Jobs keeps introducing new, unnecessary Apple products? It's not because he loves *people* but because he loves making his stock options go from $840 million to $1 billion with help from iPod, iCashIn, and i'mRich.

Hey, isn't "option" just another word for "choice?" And isn't choice what the market is all about? What *democracy* is all about? What *freedom* is all about? Freedom to make choices? Choices between options? Options among freedom?

Don't take away my freedom, man.

Options = Choices = Freedom = *America*.

## Loans: The Gift You Give Yourself

When he can't wait for his ill-gotten booty to arrive via stocks and paychecks and the broken dreams of a thousand underlings, the Great Cheater just *gives* himself money through vaguely legitimate loans. So should you. Hey, you've gotta have cash to spend on the mistress in Monte Carlo *right now!* Who can blame you?

Although they're "not supposed to," the Great Cheaters always help themselves to their company's money. I mean, you and the company are the same thing, right? *Right.* Why else would you wear a fox costume and design your accounting department to look like a henhouse?

Listen: Your happiness is the key to the success of your company. If you're spending all day worrying about how to pay for the addition to your Nantucket guest house, or whether or not your son's yacht has HBO Signature, well, that's time you won't spend making the hard decisions. Your focus won't be where it needs to be: on whatever it is you're pretending to do.

Don't worry, it's not difficult getting loans from your company. You're not borrowing from a bank with onerous "rules." Interest? Due dates? Questions about whether you really need the loan or can pay it back? *Nope, no, and, um, ah, no.*

They asked for it:

- John Rigas and family borrowed $3.1 billion from Adelphia.

- WorldCom lent $408 million to CEO Ebbers.
- Sal Giordano of Fedders got a $6 million *interest-free* loan he wouldn't have to pay off as long as he worked for the company.
- Ken Lay got a $7.5 million loan that he could repay with free company stock. *That's multitasking!*
- Mercury Interactive lent their CEO $2.4 million so he could exercise his stock options. *That's multitasking in the other direction!*

Once you borrow a boatload of money, you'll want to do three things:

1. Don't disclose the loan. At most, put it in a footnote in an appendix to an addendum to a supplemental ancillary report.
2. Ask for loan forgiveness. It doesn't work for student loans, but "emerging market" countries and Great Cheaters regularly default on their debts and are often bailed out by concerned governments and duped citizens. Why shouldn't you be?
3. Prepare this response for when you are asked to provide receipts or other paperwork: "My dog ate it." Buy a dog. Take out a loan to do so.

After you've tapped out loans, consider "doing business

with yourself."* Vernon W. Hill II, CEO of Commerce Bancorp, leased property to his bank from his real estate firm for about $2 million per year; the bank spent almost $500,000 on a golf course owned by him; and his wife runs an interior design company that billed Commerce $9.2 million in 2006. Now, if you're thinking, "Hey, all the Commerce banks look the same—she couldn't have done $9.2 million worth of work!" let me just add, "Duh." *That's how you Get Rich Cheating.*

If you can pay an outsider to do two jobs, why can't you pay an insider like yourself to do two or three or four? After all, *you're* not just the CEO, *you're* an invaluable advisor. *You've* got some kind of expertise, right? What about your wife/girlfriend/eight-year-old son? Surely they're experts in something. With a little paperwork, *you* can create a fake consulting company with the expertise any reliable advisor would say *you* need. Luckily, *you're* also that reliable advisor. *You'd* better hire *yourself* to refer *yourself* to *you* as an advisor on matters such as retaining *you* as a consultant on projects requiring *your* advice.

It's like a game of Monopoly in which you're the only player and every Chance card says, "Hire yourself, pass Go, collect $200 million, roll again." The game only ends when you have enough money to unhinge your jaw and swallow the world.

---

* *Not* a euphemism for "touching yourself," though it is just as dirty.

# Money for Nothing and Your Cheats for Free

In general, in order to Get Rich Cheating, you must "do something." The Great Cheaters don't care what and neither should you. Sell stuff, make trinkets, move things around, whatever. The more obscure, the better. Later, you'll want to say you didn't understand. To this day, no one really knows what Enron did.

*Buuuuuuuut*, there are a few exceptions, ways you can cheat yourself tons of money without really doing anything. Here are some ideas to get you started.

## Endorsements

How hard is it to say, "I like this product," and then collect hundreds of thousands of dollars? You get paid for doing nothing, for not exerting yourself in any way. Maybe you stand in front of a camera for a few minutes. Yawn.

Lance Armstrong had a deal with the U.S. Postal Service for $4 million per year, one hundred times the average postal worker's salary, and all he had to do was display the logo . . . not lose your mail, not take a break during busy times, not go on a violent rampage. Just bike wearing stickers. Tiger Woods makes $100 million each year from Nike, Titleist, Buick, Gatorade, and whoever makes hot Norwegian wives. LeBron James earns $25 million, and he's, like, seven years old. Dale Earnhardt Jr. gets about the same for slapping logos all over himself while trying to forget he's doing the same exact thing that killed his father. Kobe Bryant pockets nearly $16 million a year (though he spends a good chunk of it on "Sorry I cheated on you" jewelry). Peyton Manning can't go nineteen minutes without filming a commercial, Charlize Theron makes even watches look good, Catherine Zeta-Jones annoys you with T-Mobile ads, and no one knows why Celine Dion is allowed to live, yet she does. They're all making millions endorsing products, just being who they are, telling us to buy stuff.

## Residuals

Actors and screenwriters make money every time their performance or work appears. Not just the first time, when they're paid for it, but every time it reruns, whether it's on prime time or cable or a telenovela marathon in Portugal. You think your life is hard? Try hanging out with some clown who spoke three words in *The Shawshank Redemption*. "We get it, you're making money even as you drink, we're all very happy for you, you cheated really well—now please stop talking about what a nice guy Tim Robbins is."

## Shoot Through the Loophole

Keith Van Horn resigned from the NBA but didn't file his paperwork. In 2008, in order to satisfy salary cap needs, he was signed and traded between the Dallas Mavericks and New Jersey Nets. He never played a minute. His take for the year: $4.3 million. You might want to keep your eye out for such loophole-portunities.

# Get Rich Cheating

## Hedge Funds

Not a reserve of cash to pay your gardener, as I was led to believe, they are big green bales of cash separating the lawns of prosperity from the sidewalks of poverty. Hedge funds handle investor finances (about $1.5 trillion per year) and their managers get *at least* 1 percent of the value of the fund, *regardless of how it performs*, then another 20 percent of the profit.

Our government loves hedge funds too. In February 2007, the Bush administration said there was no need for greater government oversight of the industry, and many funds—like Pequot Capital Management,* the Quellos Group,** and Amaranth Advisors†—have enjoyed the "Congress doesn't want to investigate us because of our political connections" cushion.

So, easy pickings:

Manage a $1 billion hedge fund and get 1 percent ($10 million) off the top. If you make no money, take that $10 million. *Or*, lie and say the fund made $100 million; then take 20 percent ($20 million) of that. *Or*, steal the whole $1 billion, and take the $10 million too. What do you do later when people question your numbers? That's right, you restate your past financials, declare bankruptcy, get immunity from

---

* Managed by connected people who, whoops, can't be interviewed by the SEC.

** Described as a maker and seller of abusive tax shelters that helped five wealthy clients shield $2 billion in taxes.

† This fund basically bet that another hurricane would affect gas prices . . . and it lost about $4.2 billion. I haven't seen a hurricane cause this much damage since Jimmy Johnson left the University of Miami.

your congressional friends, and move to Turks and Caicos! *Hooray!**

You'll be the envy of your smarter, more experienced, harder-working friends. Your *poor* friends.

---

* This maneuver will be explained further in Chapter 18.

## IO

# Undertake the Underlings

## You Can Screw *Some* of the People *All* of the Time . . .

Once you've figured out how much you'll get paid, you will need to hire a bunch of suckers to help you "do your job," whatever that is. There are hundreds of books on managing employees, but none on exploiting them. Why is that? Must be because everyone is afraid of getting rich. You, on the other hand, are the bravest person in the world.

In the employer-employee relationship, the balance of power is tipped in your favor: Wages are lower than thirty years ago, unions are marginalized, people work more and earn less, outsourcing threatens job security, as does immigration (a.k.a. *in*sourcing). If you like that balance, keep your thumb on the scale.

No matter when you're reading this book, there are thousands of people who want a job, who *need* a job. Remember that. Use 'em and lose 'em. There are always more. What if we run out? Well, India isn't just for curry anymore.

# Undertake the Underlings

Exploit your employees.

Cheatable employees aren't just the nine-to-five schmucks in your office. They're the maids at whom you throw your cell phone, the underage congressional pages you inappropriately appropriate, the ball boys, the personal assistants, vice presidents, gardeners, and chauffeurs on whom you spit while counting your loot.

Get the most out of your employees through motivation tactics that overpaid consultants call "carrots" and "sticks." Carrots are rewards and incentives. Sticks are punishments. A Great Cheater uses both.

Companies, like fish, rot from the head down: The energy traders at Enron were cutthroat, mischievous, and nasty only because of the example set by their superiors. Lead by example, and you can have your own little Enron.

Encourage their greed. Flaunt your excess so underlings think it can be theirs. Wear fancy suits, talk about your money, have different mistresses "lunch" you each day. Arrive to work in a limo, chariot, or gold lamé space suit. Tell your employees, "All this can be yours, too." Spread rumors that you started in the mail room years ago even if your daddy just bought you the company last month. Offer riches and glory, promotions, bonuses, and respect if they work just a little bit harder, *but* never deliver. Keep advancement and happiness just out of their reach. Tell each employee that the *others* are putting in long hours and neglecting their families and if *they* don't, they "lack commitment." Foster jealousy. They'll strive and strive and strive and jump through all the hoops you put before them in hopes of getting money and power . . . but you'll always ask for more. Think of your promises as the electric bunny on the dog track of their career. Run them till they drop. Here are some helpful tips for instilling fear and keeping order (i.e., backstabbing) in the ranks below you.

## Fire at Will

You can fire them whenever you want, without any reason whatsoever. Make sure they know that. A daily e-mail reminder's a good start, but why not arbitrarily fire good performers so that no one feels safe? Thanks, Computer Associates—great idea.

You fire them; they don't quit on you. Citigroup requires a *fifty*-day notice before leaving. That's a good start. See how many obstacles to departure *you* can create. This way you create opportunities for—*drumroll, please*—mass firings! These aren't just tools of fear and intimidation; they're also good for the bottom line. You'll be hailed as a savior, the stock price will shoot up, and you can cash out and split.

### Mass Firing Tips

1. Do it during the holidays: Your other crimes will pale in comparison to stealing Tiny Tim's crutches.
2. Do it on the same day as CEO bonuses are announced. Distract and destroy.

3. Hire security guards to make sure everyone leaves peacefully and to confiscate the "Hang in There!" cat-in-the-tree posters.

If mass firings aren't your thing, threaten outsourcing at every opportunity. Start meetings by asking, "How would Nike just do it?"

# Noncompete = Slave for Life

Put aggressive noncompete clauses like this in all employment contracts: "You cannot work anywhere else, ever, for any reason." Trust me. I'm a lawyer.*

# Spy on Them

Walmart has former CIA, FBI, and Justice Department agents trail employees. One agent pressed his ear against a bedroom wall in Guatemala to prove a manager was having an affair with a lower-level employee. *Guatemala?* Hadn't they ever heard of Motel 6? Seriously though, hats off to Walmart: If your workers flee to Central America to escape your unblinking eye, then you've clearly instilled some good fear.

---

* As part of Robert Nardelli's severance from Home Depot, he'll get another $18 million if he doesn't work for a competitor. This is the kind of noncompete you want for yourself, *not* for your employees. For your minions, stab them if they even look at another job.

## Discourage Do-Gooders

Set up an 800 number for employees to report ethics issues. Monitor it. Fire those who call. Burn down their houses.

Institute daily "team-building" exercises to eliminate individualism and institutionalize ritual humiliation. (*See* Walmart.) Break up unions (Walmart), ignore overtime laws (Walmart), and, heck, eat babies (yup . . . Walmart).

## Politicize Them

There's plenty of employee exploitation in the U.S. Congress, a.k.a. the Walmart of politics. Candidates routinely use election volunteers for career advancement. Question: Who's easier to fool: idealistic college kids or confused old people? Answer: Both. Some campaigns got Attorney General Alberto Gonzales to fire *his* subordinates for not prosecuting *their* opponents. Once in office, congressmen like Anthony Weiner abuse unpaid staff, throw phones and hissy fits, use their underlings for personal errands, and demand that they work long, hard, low-paid hours if they have any hope for a tiny taste of power.*

## Special Underling Provision: Pensions

*Nature's little piggybank.* The U.S. pension system was a post–World War II promise: Workers give their productive years to the company, and the company cares for those workers when

---

* David W. Chen, "Congressman Pushes Staff Hard, or Out the Door," *The New York Times*, July 23, 2008.

they're old. *Hmm.* I don't remember making that promise. Do *you*?

What is a pension, really? It's a system whereby your employees give you money for safekeeping. *Free money.* Sounds good to me. You know where you should keep their money? In your bank. Maybe roll it over into some nice real estate. Hey, doesn't your wife have a birthday coming up?

### *"But what happens when the employees ask for their money back?"*

Timing is everything, friend. Northwest Airlines was losing $4 million *a day* and had a $65 million payment due to its pension plan. The company had been shortchanging the pension for years but still didn't have the money. What did it do? It declared bankruptcy *the day before the payment was due*. That payment was forgotten, *and* they still brought home big CEO compensation! Nice. Then, just for kickers, when they had their mass firing, they gave laid-off employees a booklet entitled *101 Ways to Save Money*. They really did that. My favorite? *#37: Don't let the door hit you on the way out.*

So either take money out of your employee pension plan, or never put it in. Then, if they ask for it, just declare bankruptcy! It's so easy, even an airline can do it.*

---

\* A new pension "law" may require you to provide computer-based investment advice to your employees. It's not called "The Enron Provision," but it should be. Use the following high-tech computer program IF you are an employee of this company; IF you have money; IF you want more; AND you want to keep your job. THEN invest all your money in this company.

# Get Rich Cheating

Look, the pension was a gamble from the start. Gambling is an American tradition, which is why there are so many Native American casinos. Workers placed a bet that we would keep our promise. They collectively rolled the dice. Snake eyes. Craps. Losers. "Oh well, better luck next time. Here's a gold watch. Now, get off my property."

## II

# Exploit Everyone

## . . . and *All* of the People *Some* of the Time

**E**mployees aren't the only people you can use to Get Rich Cheating. America is the land of cheating opportunity, filled with many fools. The Statue of Liberty says, "Give me your tired, your poor, your huddled masses yearning to breathe free" because they're really easy to trick. Give them to me.

*Question: Who is greedy and desperate enough to be cheated?*

Athletes, students, homeowners, colleges, doctors, fans, actors, immigrants, the devout, and more.

*Better question: Who isn't greedy and desperate enough?*

No one. Take advantage of them all.

*Feeling guilty before you start?*

Well then, put down this book and pick up *Everybody Poops* because you're a big, fat baby. Whatever you do to them is no big deal: Their kids will get over it.

Now then, here are some proven *losers* that you can use to become a *winner* in the game of cheat.

## Young Athletes with Nowhere to Go

For most kids, education, college, hard work, and long-term planning aren't just unrealistic and out of reach, they're uninteresting and uninspiring. Have you talked to anyone under twenty-five lately? You'll be lucky if you get ten words in before their Sidekicks bleep-bleep their shizzle-things. Shizzeriously.

The instant riches of sports and entertainment are an escape route. A way to make it big without making a mess. Stars only seem to need natural gifts like strength, looks, speed, and a smile. *You and I* know that less than 0.000001 percent of the kids who neglect hard work in favor of pursuing fame and glory ever earn a month's rent that way, but hey, their failure isn't your concern. That's for the prison system to sort out. *(Note to self: Invest in prisons.)*

As an aspiring cheater, you must take advantage of the poor, somewhat gifted, and extremely underserved . . . just like everyone else before you. Kids today will give up their bodies and futures to chase victories, girls, and shoe deals. Why not lighten their loads by taking money off their hands?

Run a sports camp to help them "make it." Be an agent and bribe them to give you a cut. Go to the Dominican Republic and skim thousands from young shortstops' signing bonuses. Be a booster and buy them a car to go to your school.

Encourage them to live and dream beyond their means so that they are literally in debt to you. Sure, you might cost them college eligibility, but that'll just get them to big professional bucks more quickly. You're doing them a favor.

*Be a college coach.* Make promises you can't keep to recruit the best athletes to sacrifice and sweat for your program. If they help win a few games, *you* can jump from school to school, extorting gifts from admins and boosters, making and breaking million-dollar contracts with the ease and impunity of someone who, well, likes getting rich off the dreams of poor kids. *Hey! That's you* . . . and Alabama/LSU/Miami coach Nick Saban.

*Be a shoe company.* Nike and Reebok milk these young cash cows all around the athletic barn.

- First, pressure pro sports leagues to glorify individual accomplishments over team identity to enhance star power and earning potential. *Done.*
- Second, use the media to dangle the prospect of million-dollar endorsement deals and enhanced fame in front of the kids. *Check.*
- Third, while they're sacrificing other pursuits for your manufactured dream, remind them that the only way to get good enough to *endorse* your shoes is to *wear* your shoes—and jerseys and shorts and shin guards and underwear. A full outfit costs about $500, but that's just an investment in themselves.

- Fourth, keep working the media to perpetuate the cycle. *Done and done*: Sneaker ads make athletes look entertaining and clever.

Clearly, wearing your gear will make kids good at sports, get them to the pros, earn them money, book them commercials, develop their personalities, and score them babes. Heck, I want some of that! (Is there competitive napping?)

While you're at it, don't forget that college athletics is a big business. ESPN, ESPN2, ESPN Deportes, and ESPN Omnipotent provide zillion-dollar TV deals. The Bowl Championship Series, March Madness, whatever field hockey does . . . Big business, big money. Guess who gets *none* of that moola? The athletes. Leaving lots left over for you and you and you. And *you*.

College sports reek of desperation well beyond kids trying to make it big or—*gasp*—get a decent education. There's the hard-pressed athletic director looking to make a splash, a school president seeking a fund-raising edge, local politicians wanting national recognition, boosters needing to relive their brief glory days while their Stepford wives share Botox needles, and entire communities with nothing but Saturday tailgates in the parking lot of State U. Have you ever been to Lincoln, Nebraska? Outside of the local football team, there's absolutely, positively no reason to live. These folks will not just look the other way when you cheat—they'll help you make it happen.

Use time-honored traditions like recruiting scandals, fake courses, lowered academic standards, plagiarism, and fraudulent test scores. Offer coaches and recruits sex, money, cars, and fame. Even *Harvard* did it, lowering test scores for some basketball studs. (See? Smart people cheat.)

Georgia basketball coach Jim Harrick's son taught his players a course called "Coaching Principles and Strategies of Basketball." They all got As. Harrick's salary at various schools is about $750,000. He's been fired for fraud and harassment, but he keeps coaching because he knows how to win and he brings the joyous, fleeting sensation of victory to alumni and administrators alike.

Desperate folk will bend over backward for a winning sports team. *While they're down there, pick up the money that falls out of their pockets.*

## Sports Fans

Speaking of sports, don't just exploit the empty despair of athletes, colleges, and alumni—go for the fans of professional sports. These losers want to be part of a community so they can share feelings and trumped-up "knowledge" with other sad sacks around the water cooler. Rome got great by giving people bread and circuses. You don't have time to bake bread—you're trying to *make* bread,* so put a circus in your park. Raise ticket prices, introduce new team jerseys every other week, make them buy personal seat licenses, charge

---

* The money kind. Dough.

them ridiculous rates to watch their team on TV, the web, mobile devices, or sell them a small tracking chip to insert under their skin . . . with their favorite team logo!

Young fan Jeffrey Maier risked his life to grab a fly ball and help the Yankees cheat their way to a World Series title and untold riches. Where is he now? The Yankees don't care, but they're still raising ticket prices based on the World Series cachet he helped them cheat.

# College Kids

Nonathletes and non-Hiltons do believe they need a college education to do anything these days. But tuitions are sky-rocketing, scholarships and grants are being cut, and kids are desperate to . . . *dingdingdingdingding!*

College kids are so great, aren't they? Usually they're drunk or scantily clad, or, in the spring, both. They're full of confidence, believing they're indestructible and that Dane Cook is profound. They say youth is wasted on the young, but they never realized how youth could be cheated by the student loan industry. Ya see, young cheat, college kids don't shop around, read fine print, or bother worrying about tomorrow.

A wise student loan company can use a variety of means to get money from these kids: Fake checks and rebates, logos that look official, lies about which loans are available, free iPods! Student Financial Services of Clearwater, Florida paid students $50 to refer others to the company. Fifty bucks is a lot of pizza and ten-cent wings to a student who's stuck in a

$200,000 loan from Student Financial Services of Clearwater, Florida . . . *hey, wait a second!*

Or go to the "official source" and get listed as a preferred loan company by the school. You may have to grease the palm whose fingers type these lists, but it won't take much. Just give loan officers a 2 percent kickback or gifts or vacations or stock or the location of their kidnapped daughter. Whatever it takes to be the indispensable option for those who need you to fund their fruitless dreams.

Seriously, zillions of schools are under investigation for pimping student loan companies, and some, like Syracuse, Texas, and Penn, have confessed. At Columbia, a senior dean and financial aid officer made Student Loan Xpress one of that Ivy League school's "preferred lenders" for the tiny fee of a $100,000 stock sale.* If fancy-pants schools like that and the big lenders Sallie Mae and Citibank are in on the game, you should be too.

Of course, once you've locked them into these loans, relentlessly hound 'em till they pay. If he'd owed them money, student loan companies would've found Bin Laden by September 12, 2001.

Even if the kids can pay their own way, there's still room to cheat with college academics. "Teacher" is an anagram for

---

* Brian Ross, "Ivy League Official Cited in Student Loan Scandal," *The Blotter.* http://blogs.abcnews.com/theblotter/2007/04/ivy_league_offi.html. The dean, David Charlow, said, "We have worked with the Student Loan Xpress team . . . because they consistently meet the very high standards for service that our students and parents expect," then added, "Whaddaya gonna do about it, bitches?"

"cheater." Coincidence? I cheat not. The president of Oral Roberts University—Richard Roberts, son of the televangelist Oral Roberts (family tradition!)—mobilized students to campaign for a mayoral candidate, had his house remodeled eleven times in fourteen years, coerced underlings to lie to the IRS, flew the school jet to family vacations, and used school funds to pay for cell phones, including text messages sent to hot undergrad boys between one and three a.m. *Really.* Hey, no one ever said Get Rich Cheating wasn't compatible with Be a Creep Cheating.

Is it an abuse of trust for a college to let a student loan lender use the school logo so that it looks official? *Perhaps.* But . . . doesn't that lender give some of its ill-gotten money back to the school and officials who made it all possible? *Yes.* So, what's the problem?

## Doctors with Bills to Pay

Sure, health care is expensive for patients, but it's also costly for your neighborhood docs. They have malpractice insurance, staff, student loans, second homes, and ex-wives to pay. (The working title for *ER* was *Desperate Doctors*.) They need a little extra money. So, medical services provider, give them that *little* extra to help cheat yourself *a lot* more. Bribe doctors, medical researchers, and hospitals to push your product onto patients and peers through fake studies, endorsements, and "off-label" uses.

Half the doctors in a study promoting Prodisc (an artificial spinal disk) over vertebrae-fusing surgery for lower-back pain had financial stakes in the success of the product, through funds operated by a company called Viscogliosi Brothers.* Ephedra's a weight-loss drug that killed hundreds (including baseball player Steve Belcher), but doctors kept pushing it on patients because Wellness International Network kept pushing money on doctors.** Neurontin was approved by the FDA to treat epilepsy. It was also "approved" to treat migraines, bipolar disorder, and low funds by wise doctors willing to sign off on research articles they didn't write just for a small honorarium and a twinkle in the eye.† No need for fancy clinical drug trials—just fill this specimen cup with cash.

How do you bribe doctors, er, "medical professionals?" Pay for them to "consult," give them cash "grants" for "studies," send them on exotic trips to "seminars" and "prostitutes," and use former cheerleaders as product salespeople. Heck, nothing brightens a doctor's day after thirty-two cases of leprosy like a miniskirt and pompoms. And a brightened day means more referrals for he who shed the light.

## Creative Types

Exploit needy actors, writers, and women with father issues who want to be on TV. Make them pay for acting lessons or to meet "industry," charge $500 for a head shot they could

---

\* Reed Abelson, "Financial Ties Are Cited as Issue in Spine Study," *The New York Times*, January 30, 2008.

\*\* David Callahan, *The Cheating Culture*, p. 51.

† Ibid, pp. 9, 52–56.

take for free on their digital camera, take 15 percent of the earnings they themselves worked to secure, or sleep with them . . . and make millions off the resulting sex tape.

Ooh, ooh, here's an idea: Start a service that offers downloads of original content. Prey on the creative community's economic despair. Have them provide original content—hopefully their life's work—and grant yourself exclusive, perpetual ownership rights in all media. Promise them "exposure." When one million people download it for $10 each, laugh, laugh, laugh as the creators die alone, poor, and obscure.

## The Talentless, Stupid, and Blonde . . .

. . . are who beauty pageants, reality television, *Girls Gone Wild*, and porn are for. Make money off them. The porn industry recently threatened to relocate if California raised taxes on it. The adult entertainment industry works because all the "actors" believe that, by being near Hollywood, they are, in fact, in the real "entertainment industry" and not "very, very sad." As for reality television, what's the *only* difference between that and what I just said about porn? *Less pants*.

## Soldiers and Their Sympathizers

What about soldiers fighting for our country? They're dying for your freedom to cheat, and their money's just as green as anyone else's.

The Coalition to Salute America's Heroes, a charity to

help wounded veterans, collected $160 million between 2004 and 2006. What did they do with that money? About $125 million went to salaries, fund-raising, and perks like golf club memberships. That's an incredible 75 percent cheating! *Bravo!* General Tommy Franks got a cool $100,000 for endorsing the charity. The head of the company got $1.5 million in salary and more than $300,000 in expenses, a home . . . *and it was all legal!* Charities like this don't have to disclose to donors where the money goes! *Yee-haw!*

> **In$piration:** *"If we disclose [where the money went], which I'm more than happy to do, we'd all be out of business. Nobody would donate. It would dry up."*
> —Roger Chapin, founder of the Coalition to Salute America's Heroes, testifying before a House committee*

## Immigrants

They'll work for below minimum wage and won't complain because the politicians you've bribed have scared them to death with deportation campaigns. They'll pick produce, clean bathrooms, and raise your kids for pennies a day! Or . . . you could become a border agent, take massive bribes to smuggle human life, lock people in airless trucks, spend their money, and perhaps remember them someday when it's really hot.

---

* "An Intolerable Fraud," *The New York Times,* February 8, 2008. Well . . . *duh.*

Immigrant exploitation in politics is nothing new either. Tammany Hall's power was based on New York's immigrant population, which was grateful for the not-exactly-legit services that the regime provided the underserviced. In exchange for loyalty and votes (and votes and votes), Tammany Hall provided the poor with food, heat, jobs, rent, a social network, and the means to interact with the new world. See, if they knew how to exploit in the nineteenth century, you should too. If it ain't broke, don't fix it. *If it ain't broke, you won't be either.*

## Christians

Good, honest people who believe in a greater power are sheep whose financial fleece you must shear with phony divinity. Invite them to your church, pass out the tithing tray, get tax breaks and homages, tune their TVs to your televangelism, and rake in the millions. Put a price on salvation and open up the cash register.

John Hagee made millions; Jim and Tammy Faye Bakker used makeup to frighten billions more; Jimmy Swaggart, Jerry Falwell, Joel Osteen, and the like bring in the big-believing bucks. Priest Rodney Rodis embezzled between $600,000 and $700,000 from St. Jude Catholic Church and Immaculate Conception Catholic Church in Virginia by telling parishioners to mail donations to a post office box he controlled. Then he just transferred the money to a bank account. *How simple is that?*

Just be a spiritual leader who takes your flock to a safe

deposit box. Churchgoers pray for miracles. Sometimes they happen. For you. *Prai$e the Lord!*

## Nonprofits

Charity: It's not just for the poor anymore. You need some too. America has a great tradition of philanthropy and public service that Great Cheaters exploit to get rich. I'm not just talking about fake tax deductions.

You know what a real Great Cheater does? Creates his own charity to push the cheating envelope. Filling out 501(c)(3) nonprofit incorporation paperwork is easy. Just say you love puppies or the environment or kids, make a couple copies, and stick it in the mail.

King Pharmaceuticals created the King Benevolent Fund, which took outdated meds and redistributed them to poor African countries where the dating restrictions aren't as rigid and, apparently, the lives aren't worth as much. Of course, when the good people at King wanted to increase their corporate earnings, they just "sold" a dizzillion useless drugs to the Benevolent Fund at ridiculously high prices. *Allegedly.* That's why they called them "King."

So donate products, overinflate their value,* take a charitable tax deduction, and hey, why not book billions of dollars in goodwill? ("Goodwill" is not where you donate old clothes, but an intangible measure of your reputation. It's like karma, but more bankable.)

---

* *See:* Every donation ever made, ever. Yes, Goodwill-that-accepts-clothing, those socks were worth $13,000.

Again, feeling bad about starving children is no excuse to stop exploiting them. Once you've made billions, you can build a hospital or adopt Madonna's babies or do whatever you need to do to kill your conscience.

$ $ $

I've tossed out a lot of possible exploitees, but a Great Cheater knows this is just the tip of the iceberg. We didn't even get to the elderly, floating on leaking life rafts next to the iceberg that sunk their ship. Do anything you want to old people. They love the attention and might even think you're related!

There are *just so many* gullible people from whom you can scam enough money to add a ski house onto your beach house. Don't believe me? Go to a public place, my young cheating friend. Look around. Everyone you see is unhappy. Everyone you see is poor. Everyone you see would do anything to be happy and rich. Take advantage of them all, for *their* own good, and *your* own cheat.

# 12

# Accomplices and Enablers

## You Got Friends in Low Places

Successful professionals are part of a great team. Successful cheaters *exploit* a great team. No matter who you're taking advantage of—whether you're cheating employees, voters, sports fans, or residents of convalescent homes—you want to make sure that you surround yourself with the best accomplices available, from trainers to entourages, congressional staffers to boards of directors, accountants, auditors, editors, boosters, and even a complicit golf caddy. If they can metaphorically or literally warm up the getaway car, give them the metaphorical keys (unless you left them on the metaphorical nightstand again).

What makes a good accomplice?

I'm glad you asked. *Loyalty above all else.* Greg Anderson was willing to go to jail to protect Barry Bonds. Bernie Kerik buried bodies (figuratively?) for Rudy Giuliani. Lucifer takes the rap for God's bad days. These are good accomplices, and here are a few more that you'll need if you're going to make this work.

## Muscle

It never hurts to have some tough guys around who can break a couple legs or arrange some swims-with-fishes. Doesn't matter if they're actually mob characters like Bernie Kerik or "legitimate businessmen" like Anthony Pellicano—private investigator for stars like Chris Rock, Steven Segal, and Brad Grey—or just guys named Vito and Tony. A picture's worth a thousand words, but a busted face is worth a million . . . and usually costs only half as much.

## Braaaaains

Science isn't just a vast left-wing conspiracy, nor is it only to be used when a couple teenage boys want to conjure Kelly LeBrock. Science is there for you. BALCO—the Bay Area Laboratory Co-Operative—designed the untraceable new steroid known as THG. Run by cartoonishly mustachioed Victor Conte, this "co-operative" has been linked to many of the Great Cheaters of our time, including Barry Bonds, Marion Jones, Jason Giambi, Gary Sheffield, Bill Romanowski, and Jason Grimsley. So follow the trail of pitchforks and torches to your local mad scientist and ask if he and his hunchbacked assistant have any new potions to help you become the belle of the next Young Republicans Ball.

## Money Men

You're going to need investors to make some of your cheating plans happen. If you can't just steal your start-up capital, recruit some heavy hitters. Look to those with a reputation for skirting the rules so you know they're cool with your cheating . . . and won't be surprised when you don't pay them back. Norman Hsu is a big Democratic Party power broker and donor who raised almost $1 million for Hillary Rodham Clinton. Give him a call . . . once he gets out of jail for running a Ponzi scheme.*

## "Friends"

Keep your friends close, but keep your coconspirators closer. While most of the folks in this chapter are good accomplices, some become snitches, which are what we call "bad accomplices." Drug dealers, for example, aren't trustworthy. *Shocking.* Yes, you gotta get your fix somewhere, and a *professional* drug dealer is safer than cruising the 'hood for a dime bag of HGH. But for every honorable Greg Anderson, there are ten Brian McNamee, a former cop who kept old syringes, bloody gauze, and records of injections and abscesses in butts. He

---

* A Ponzi scheme should not be confused with a *Fonzi scheme*, which is when you hang around Arnold's drive-in with Ralph Malph and Richie Cunningham. (A Fonzi scheme, in turn, shouldn't be confused with a Chachi situation or a Mr. C. scenario.) It's just a pyramid racket where investors make money from subsequent investors with no real product. Before Bernie Madoff, a famous case was Refco, whose futures division was forced to declare bankruptcy. That's a beautiful metaphor for our world: The future is bankrupt, the past is fleeting, and the present is imaginary. Perfect reasons to Get Rich Cheating right now.

ratted out Andy Pettitte, who ratted out Roger Clemens, who ratted out his wife . . . who swallowed the spider to catch the fly . . . I don't know why she swallowed the fly—perhaps she thought it was THG.

Snitches are sad, deceitful, and disloyal. Whether they're doing it to sell books (Jose Canseco, Bush White House confidants Scott McClellan and Richard Clarke and Christine Whitman and Lawrence Lindsey and Paul Bremer, et cetera, *ad infinitum*), for revenge (prep basketball star OJ Mayo's former friend Louis Johnson), self-preservation (McNamee and Andy Pettitte), ego (former Patriots cameraman Matt Walsh and assistant coach Eric Mangini), or victory (Red Sox director George Mitchell fingering Yankees players, Republicans nailing Alabama governor Don Siegelman, and everyone who's ever lost the Tour de France), steer clear of them. If it looks like your accomplices might become snitches, either ask them to wait until you've cheated enough loot to flee the country, or just arrange for "an accident." (*See above,* Muscle.)

Friends don't always work out, but so what? You're not here to make friends, you're not here to keep friends—you're here to get rich.

## Lovers

On the other hand, the closest of friends, your lovers, can prove quite useful. Tonya Harding's chubby hubby Jeff Gillooly arranged a knee-whack attack on Nancy Kerrigan, which, in turn, gave Harding the 1990 U.S. Championship and a lucrative career in has-been boxing and being a professional train wreck. Marion Jones was an expert at picking mates who'd maximize her cheating potential:

- She married shot-putter CJ Hunter in 1997, who introduced her to the coach, Trevor Graham, who helped her get several gold medals at the 2000 Olympics with PEDs.
- After divorcing Hunter, in 2003 she had Tim Montgomery's son.
- The Tim-ster was banned from track and field for steroid use *and* convicted in a bank fraud scheme, which also involved Jones.

Hey, this is some careful planning by Miss Marion! She must've been internet dating on Match.ex-con.

## Personal Advisers

Every czar needs a Rasputin. Karl Rove is the gold standard for advisors to the cheaters. His brilliant manipulation of reality helped George Bush "win" two elections and pass untold piles of legislation that enhanced the cheating wealth of a nation. Other well-known advisers to the cheats include parents (*hello,* Lynn Spears, Dina Lohan, Queen Elizabeth), confidants (*bonjour,* Linda Tripp), and obscure political experts (*buenos días,* John Ehrlichman). Just be ready, young cheat, to cut your advisers loose once they become a liability or their advice ceases to produce re$ults or your fourteen-year-old sister gets pregnant. Loyalty is a one-way street, heading only in your direction. The other way leads to Poorville. Population: Them.

## Machine Politicians

"Machine politics" hasn't been in the news much since Tammany Hall and Chicago's Democratic mayor Richard J. Daley, but it's still in play. Use patronage positions to generate support among an army of local leaders who'll ensure continued electoral victories and the passage of laws that'll enrich those who really matter: you and your cheating chums.

## Professionals

There are, of course, professional, institutional, legitimate accomplices you can hire to enable you. Tax firms exist primarily to help you avoid paying taxes. *They've said so under oath.* The accounting firm KPMG created inappropriate shelters for wealthy individuals:

> *"[The tax shelters] were allegedly designed to create phony losses that investors could use to reduce their taxes . . . The IRS contends that all these loans and investments were risk-free, sham transactions designed solely to reduce taxes—to the tune of nearly $12 billion in phony losses that cost the Treasury $2.5 billion."*

---

\* "Inside the KPMG Mess," *Business Week*, September 12, 2005.

*That was their job!* They obviously know what they're doing, so hire them, listen to them, put everything in their name, and blame them later. Unless, of course, you don't want to Get Rich Cheating. *Do you?*

## Auditors/Consultants

Let us now, aspiring cheat, bow our heads in a moment of silence for Arthur Andersen. Artie. The big one. The troublemaker from back in the day. You remember the good times, right? Back when a man was a man and an auditor was a consultant. *Damn!* Gives me shivers just to think about it. Yeah, Artie was unbeatable . . . in the zone . . . like Jordan, Brady, and Tiger all in one. Artie got millions of dollars to offer advice and consulting to nice companies like Enron. Then it got millions more from, say, Enron, to audit, say, Enron's activities, which were largely based upon the advice and consultation Artie had provided. For some strange reason, the audits never said the advice was bad. *I $$ can't $$ imagine $$ why $$*.

Sure, Artie got busted. As did Enron. But, really, what's a national scandal between friends?

**Succes$tory:** *"Now we're 'Accenture.'"*

—Arthur Andersen

**Succes$tory:** *"And I'm 'dead.'"*

—Ken Lay

Consulting services have made up the bulk of revenues for most of the Big Five accounting firms.* Yes, Great Cheaters have one company give them advice and the same company audit the results of that advice. CEOs even have these companies consult with them about how much money they should make.**

**CHEAT CHAT**

. . . . . . . . . . . . . . . . . . . . . . . . . . . . . . . . . .

You might worry that the powers that be would try to stop this conflict of interest. Um, obviously you've never met the powers that be. Let me introduce you: Open a wallet—whether it's yours or not—and take out some bills. Now look at the names and faces of the powers that be.

So, hire someone to advise you how to cheat; then have that same someone certify that cheating. Ask point-blank, "Is that cheating?" What do you think he'll say? (Make sure you're holding your pen over his paycheck when you ask.)

---

\* Alex Berenson, *The Number,* p. 123.
\*\* A House panel found massive conflicts of interest among executive compensation consultants. "Consultants who do other work for companies while helping them devise executive pay recommended significantly higher pay packages than" those that didn't have such relationships, prompting reactions ranging from "Duh" to "No duh."

Still having trouble understanding this? Okay, imagine your wedding anniversary is approaching. You go to your friend Tony for advice. You say to him, "Hey, Tony, I need $10,000 to buy my wife a nice necklace. I'll give you a hundred bucks if you advise me about legitimate ways I can get it."

Tony says, "Hey, you, guy, you should hijack a cigarette truck and sell the goods on the black market. Thanks for the C-note."

You want to make sure this is sound advice, so you turn to the other guy in his Brooklyn auto shop, Tony's brother Vito. "Vito," you say. "Here's fifty clams. Is Tony's advice on the up and up?"

"Sure, boss, and for another fifty, I know a guy who can do it."

## The Ultimate Accomplice: The Board of Directors

The corporate cheat knows that the board of directors is the single most important creation in the history of the universe. Yes, *even more than space travel*. Why? Because they help you cheat yourself rich.

Directors are supposed to advise the humble CEO and oversee the company. They're *supposed to* keep questionable practices in check. *Or . . .* they come to meetings, get stoned, play Six Degrees of Kevin Bacon, and sign off on whatever you want.

The board of Take-Two Interactive—maker of wholesome fare like *Grand Theft Auto: Vice City*—admitted it was complicit in inappropriate options granting and the murder of countless cartoon hookers. Let's be honest (not something I usually condone). Although directors theoretically keep you from cheating, in reality, they're the ones who come up with the ideas in the first place.

## Who's on Board?

Who's got a better understanding of your vision and goals than other Great Cheaters? *No one.* Sit on one another's boards. Ken Lay was on Eli Lilly's board, Dennis Kozlowski on Raytheon's, even squeaky-clean Johnson & Johnson CEO Ralph Larsen was on the boards of Xerox, AT&T, and GE.* A recent study showed that CEOs whose directors sat on multiple boards were paid 13 percent more than those whose directors did not.** It takes a Great Cheater to help a Great Cheater.

Some claim these arrangements are incestuous, which explains why WorldCom had webbed feet.

Who else should be on your board? People close to you—or in your debt—are sure to have your best interests at heart. John Rigas's sons sat on Adelphia's board and kept agreeing to all his scams. Your brother-in-law, Tim—he's a slacker. That

---

\* Arianna Huffington, *Pigs at the Trough.*
\*\* James Surowiecki, "The Sky-High Club," *The New Yorker*, January 22, 2007. Worship Home Depot for the delicious $210 million severance received by Robert Nardelli: Eight of ten directors were CEOs at other companies and sat on an average of two other boards; the chairman of the compensation committee sat on *four* other boards; and, as soon as shareholders began to grumble, the directors simply changed their own rules about mandatory retirement so they could remain in power.

guy from the bar who owes you four hundred bucks. What about your wife? She kept her maiden name so it'll look like she's unrelated. Good.

Shockingly, even in our regulation-happy, post–financial meltdown modern era, there are surprisingly few rules about the board of directors. There's no minimum number and the only intelligence requirement is that a director understand financial statements. Here's a financial statement anyone can understand: "Do what I say and I'll give you money."

## Committees

Most of the work of the board of directors is done through committees—audit, compensation, hiring, nominating, secret slush fund creating. Each and every committee should include all the same people.* You don't want any confusion, mixed signals, or independent thought. The people who make a decision should be the people who review that decision, approve that decision, pay for that decision, approve that payment, hire someone to execute that payment, approve that hiring, and skim 10 percent off the top of the whole damn thing.

## Control

How can you control a board of directors that might, inconceivably, challenge you?

---

* Mr. Jerry Obey-the-Law wouldn't want the same people on each committee because the people who approve payments shouldn't audit those approvals. He'd want to insulate the different board functions from each other. You know what? Jerry is a filthy, stupid bastard. *Shut up, Jerry.*

- Spy on them. Hewlett-Packard's CEO Patricia Dunn hired private investigators to illegally obtain the phone records of directors in order to determine who was aligning against her. *Paranoia, self-emloy-ah.*

- Remind directors that they never ever *ever* get in trouble. Well, usually not. At least not Adelphia's board or WorldCom's or, well . . . just tell them not to worry, have them sign a waiver, and guarantee to indemnify them.* Then secretly put everything in their names.

- Use psychological warfare to make them feel inferior. Have 'em wear oversized suits and sit in really big, low chairs at a very high boardroom table. Serve warm milk and cookies. Start meetings with, "Your mother and I are very disappointed . . ."

- It's called "bribery." Any red-blooded director will patriotically ignore your $200 million theft for a $2 million "honorarium." Don't forget to write off the bribe as a business expense.

- Another one's called "blackmail." Have the goods on 'em. Throw a party, bring in recreational drugs, fake a murder, videotape the whole thing. Send 'em a copy on DVD. You saw *The Firm*, right? Channel your inner Gene Hackman.

- Try this take on the classic financial statement: "If you *don't* do what I say, I'll take away all your money, burn down your house, hunt your children, and eat your parents' kidneys." See if they understand that.

---

* Not a guarantee.

## The Times, They Might Be A-Changin'
## (But Probably Aren't)

After the scandals of the early 2000s and the financial collapse of 2008, corporate directors are, supposedly, "independent."* So directors take their jobs more seriously? *Not exactly.* Does a troll become a fairy just because they paint the bridge under which he lives? No, he just works harder to lure little Dutch children. Likewise, I'm pretty sure the board of directors will remain capable of dereliction for money.

The Great Cheater knows that, in the end, directors are human beings, made of flesh and blood, sugar and spice and everything nice, snakes and snails and puppy dog tails, the unquenchable thirst for money, and the undeniable will to feign ignorance. Use your board of directors as all the Great Cheaters have before you: to give your actions legitimacy and to give yourself wealth *ill*egitimately. It's both a tongue twister and a double-edged sword. That's why the board of directors is so important.

---

* The number of new independent directors of S&P 500 companies was up 17 percent in 2006 and 41 percent in the past five years. Don't worry: (a) I won't use genuine facts and figures like this often; and (b) you can define "independent" however you like. "Not employed by the SEC" is what the CED (Cheaters English Dictionary) uses. Plenty of room for spouses, neighbors, friends, cardboard cutouts, and those dummies people put in the passenger seat so they can use the HOV lane.

# THE ONLY MINUTES FROM A BOARD OF DIRECTORS MEETING YOU'LL EVER NEED

## PUBLIC DOCUMENT

### *Oversight Committee of the Board of Directors*
### *of Important Company*

| | |
|---|---|
| 8:30 | Opening Prayer |
| 8:45 | Pledge of Allegiance |
| 8:50 | Each director pours own decaf. |
| 9:00 | Read minutes of previous meeting. Confirmed, approved, certified in triplicate. |
| 9:30–1:30 | Presentation of issues. Intense, conscientious deliberation. All members ask pointed questions, management provides certified documentation with hand on Bible. Consider impact on stockholders, employees, environment, national security, and the spotted owl. |
| 1:30–1:45 | Brows furrowed, "harrumphs" harrumphed. |
| 1:45–4:45 | Break for yoga and organic salad, dressing on the side. |
| 4:45–5:00 | Approval of totally legal, ethical, and fair decisions discussed earlier. |
| 5:00 | Closing prayer, choose charity to receive profits. |

## PRIVATE (REAL) MINUTES OF ACTUAL MEETING
### *Board Meeting!*
See No Evil, Hear No Evil, Speak No Evil

| | |
|---|---|
| 9-ish | Check golf bags with cute receptionist. |
| 9:05 | Ask assistant to fax written apology to receptionist for inappropriate comments. |
| 9:09 | Ask other assistant to terminate first assistant and receptionist. |
| 9:12 | Scones! |
| 9:42 | CEO presents documents for approval. All but signature line blacked out. |
| 9:43 | Distribution of small bags of unmarked bills. |
| 9:48 | Muffins! |
| 9:55–10:10 | Conference call with CNBC personality (cousin of CFO) to tell him what to report. |
| 10:14 | Oh great, Murray's drunk again. |
| 10:30–11:15 | Discuss merits of Szechuan House v. Hunan Garden, difference between egg roll and spring roll. |
| 11:17 | Lunch ordered. |
| 11:21 | Champagne popped, window damaged. |
| 12:16 | Stupid plum sauce all over my tie. |
| 2:15 | Finish lunch, call restaurant, complain about incorrect order, demand refund. |
| 2:20 | Ceremonial lighting of cigars with hundred-dollar bills and/or union contract. |
| 2:50–3:25 | Watch PriceWaterhouseCoopers consulting video on stealing lollipops from babies. |

| 3:26–3:45 | Book $100 million profit from watching video. |
| 3:50 | Hookers! |
| 4:02 | Naps. |
| 4:52 | Ritual cleansing. High priest, pentagram, robes, virgin charged to corporate account. |
| 5:00 | Closing prayer, choose charity to raid. |

# 13

## Numbers Never Lie

### They Cheat

You've picked a handful of connected, sleazy scumbags to help you pull this all off. Now it's time to meet the greatest accomplice of all: numbers.

What is a number? Just a randomly chosen squiggly line representing an arbitrary quantity? *No!* Numbers are a cheater's best friend. Best friends support *you*, give *you* authority, and do the dirty work necessary for *you* to make it big—whether it's lying to an auditor, deceiving an investor, or hooking up with the hot chick's ugly girlfriend. Numbers defend the indefensible. *Nine out of ten experts agree!** 

## Batting Average = Cheating Average

Numbers help the athletic Great Cheater play, win, and get paid. Duffers fudge their golf score to impress a client or win a bet; a hit is ruled an error, giving a pitcher a lower ERA

---

* The tenth expert? Dead.

and a higher salary; Danny Almonte changed his passport birthday from 1987 to 1989 so he could pretend to be twelve and kick some Little League butt. Hey, *never* pick on someone your own size.

Sports *teams* play numeric jujitsu with the salary cap in order to both win games and screw players. In three 1997 contracts, the San Francisco Fraud Squad (a.k.a. the 49ers) secretly agreed to lower salaries of star players, with promises to pay for "future services." One got a "six-year contract" with a letter voiding the last year in order to prorate the signing bonus against the cap over six years instead of five. The biggest shock: Each player received an unlimited lifetime supply of sourdough bread and cable car rides valued at nearly $26.

Numbers don't just help franchises. A Great Cheater interprets numbers to his advantage during contract negotiations. In Major League Baseball arbitration hearings, statistics are twisted to make someone look like either the second coming of Joe DiMaggio or the fifth cousin of Marilyn Monroe. It's amazing how a player's performance, scrutinized to within a billionth of a point, can be interpreted by two smart people in two different ways, resulting in two different salaries, millions of dollars apart. This is true even though baseball is an obsessively statistical game where they practically quantify the saline content of each player's sweat when batting with two strikes, in the late innings, against a submariner, with men in scoring position, in a day game after a night game after which he cheated on his wife. (A-Rod's hitting .321 in such situations.)

MLB itself tweaks digits to its monetary advantage, testifying before Congress in 2005 that the number of positive drug tests had fallen from 2003 to 2004. True-*ish*. You see, testing was shut down for much of 2004, so there was less of a chance to get positives. Clever, clever baseball. Keep racking up the ticket sales and TV deals on the broad, rippling backs of your home run kings.

So what is the consequence of manipulating numbers in athletic competition? Being a champion who gets huge contracts and endorsement deals. Nice. To paraphrase Great Cheaters Nike and Al Davis: *Just do it, baby*.

## Numbers Rule, So Rulers Can Numb

Politics provides numerical cheating excellence in many forms. There's the magical math of elections where *more* votes for a candidate actually means *less* votes for that candidate. Al Gore got 50,499,897 "yeas" in his bid for president; George W. Bush got just around 50,456,002. That, plus the "numbers" of 271 electoral votes, 10,000 old Jews who voted for Pat Buchanan, 537 un-hanging chads in Florida, 5 Supreme Court justices, and a 2.4 percent "broad, nationwide victory" in 2004 gave us eight great years of Bush cheatership, and W's pals got to raid the Treasury.

Bush cheated everyone rich through his big 2001 tax cut, the focus of plenty of numerical distortions. The same basic figures were interpreted to mean either there'd be a $1.6 trillion cut that would spur the economy and give everyone the ability to fly, or that only thirteen people would get all the benefits and then would literally send bile and spite trickling down onto the rest of America, all while eating children who'd otherwise be forced into French, communist, gay slavery. Neither was quite true, though my twelve friends and I have enjoyed your delicious offspring.

Twisted numbers and misstated predictions distort the cost of all government programs, based solely on political position. Depending on whether or not you want to cut Medicare, Social Security, defense spending, Alaskan bridges, or Iraqi invasions, the programs are either cripplingly expensive or bargains that will pay for themselves with oil revenue. No one questions the numbers when you're trying to pass the budget or a bill. It's only afterward that the pesky Government Accountability Office tells everyone the "real" cost. By that point, no one cares. *That's* how a bill becomes a law, and you cheat yourself another $10 million in campaign contributions.

That doesn't even begin to cover the political misuse of statistics. Rudy Giuliani loved to stretch the numerical truth. During his short 2008 presidential campaign, he attempted to debunk universal health care by saying, "My chance of surviving prostate cancer . . . in the United States? Eighty-two percent . . . In England? Only 44 percent under socialized medicine."*Actually, it's 74.4 percent in Britain, and it's not socialized medicine, but those statistical misstatements did help Rudy almost make it past *three whole* primaries.

---

* Julie Bosman, "Giuliani's Prostate Cancer Figure Is Disputed," *The New York Times*, October 31, 2007.

Rudy notoriously tweaked stats to quantify his success as mayor too. They were courageously inaccurate, whether about crime, budgets, or achievements.

**In$piration:** *"All of these statements are incomplete, exaggerated, or just plain wrong."*[*]

Everyone lies about stats, but he made it a central part of his campaign. Unfortunately for him, old folks in Florida can count, even if they can't vote.

He wasn't the only 2008 candidate to play with numbers. Hillary Clinton said financing for the National Institutes of Health had decreased under George W. Bush—it hadn't. Barack Obama said national debt doubled under W—it hadn't. Still, they were just saying what they needed to say to get elected and start doling out the cash.

There's a site for confirming the "facts" presented by politicians, conveniently called FactCheck.org. Don't go there. In fact, just to help your fellow cheaters, you should buy that website and replace it with elder porn.

# Accounting 101 and Accounting 666

This is it. Accounting. The mother lode of cheating numbers. The other scams in this book can make you *some* money, but the Great Cheaters know using accounting tricks can make

---

[*] Michael Cooper, "Citing Statistics, Giuliani Misses Time and Again," *The New York Times*, November 30, 2007.

you filthy, filthy rich. And isn't that what you really want? To be covered in dirty, dirty money?

*Carpe dinero. Seize the cash.*

The lessons herein apply to every industry, because every industry must account for its riches. It's all about "creative accounting," a mystical phrase coined by the cheating gods.* "Earnings management," "aggressive accounting," "innovative numbers shenanigans," "lying" . . . these are all pretty ways of saying, "Mess with the numbers, fatten the wallet."

Don't be intimidated—accounting isn't hard. It just *seems* hard so that the average folk don't get involved, don't look behind the curtain and see the bald man with glasses stealing millions from Dorothy and the Tin Man. (Melt him down and sell him as silver.) Remember, even if *you* don't understand, you can pay someone to understand (and take the fall) for you.

Numerical smokescreens are why accounting is such a great way to Get Rich Cheating. It may not be sexy, hot, or fun, but it will get you the money to buy yourself hot, sexy fun. Investors and regulators don't have the time to examine the details of your financial statements, to parse your underlying fundamentals, your footnotes, your cross-referenced hullabaloo. So, like those before you, take advantage of their laziness to account yourself rich.

Great Cheaters account however they want, because they can. Sure, there's this thing called "GAAP"—Generally Ac-

---

* Some say it was first used in Mel Brooks's *The Producers*. I have it on bad authority that Brooks actually stole that from *the* Arthur Andersen, who was doing Brooks's taxes at the time.

cepted Accounting Principles—but as any proper exec will tell you, GAAP is for sissies. There's no law saying you have to adhere to accounting standards, so conforming is strictly a matter of personal integrity. "Personal integrity?" Never heard of it.*

Why must you use accounting to misrepresent the fi-

## CHEAT CHAT

A couple things you should know about accounting:

1. There are two accounting methods: cash and accrual. Being able to say, "We use an accrual method of accounting," will make investors think you're passably competent.**
2. "Booking" is an accounting term referring to when you enter something in your accounting "book" or "volume of bound paper with ink impressions." It's also what Danno did to the perps on *Hawaii Five-0*.

---

\* If you're asked to keep "complete and accurate" records, just buy a rubber stamp that says "complete and accurate" and use it on all your paperwork. Take out an illegal loan to pay for it.

\** The difference between cash and accrual accounting is basically whether or not you fully recognize transactions when they happen (accrual) or when they're paid for (cash). Book now or book later.

nances of your company? Because if things are "going well," you'll get a performance bonus, people will invest in you, your stock price will jump, your options will increase, and you'll Get Rich Cheating.

Bernie Ebbers made about a zillion dollars in performance pay at WorldCom, just by using accounting gimmicks to conceal $4 billion in company expenses in order to boost the bottom line. Four billion dollars? *Puh-leeze. You can cheat better than that.*

## Numbers Can Act Too

In entertainment, they even have a special term for how they make so much money: "Hollywood accounting." Put on your accountant's hat. You know, the one with the green visor. But put it on . . . *dramatically.*

During the 2007–2008 Hollywood writers' strike, the Alliance of Motion Picture and Television Producers (AMPTP) harnessed the cheating power of numbers. The AMPTP simultaneously told writers that internet content was not producing any profit and told investors that internet content was worth $500 million. Takes a truly gifted entertainer-cheater to talk out of both sides of his ass like that.

Movie distribution is a notoriously awesome type of Hollywood accounting. Distributors make sure they have "costs" equal to their income so there's nothing left for anyone who gets a share of net profit. They do it by excluding certain revenue or just making up expenses.

You'd think it'd be hard to cheat like that on big hits

everyone knows must be raking it in. Remember the block-buster *Lord of the Rings* trilogy? Well, its producer—New Line Cinema—allegedly didn't make any money because the company didn't pay the Tolkien estate anything. Makes sense to me. I'm sure it was really expensive for New Line to spend all the money it cheated. I mean, currency conversion from Elvish to dollars *alone* probably siphoned off a few million Frodos.

# 14

## Hire the Numbers

### Don't Need a Signing Bonus, Corner Office, or Health Care!

All right! Enough tiptoeing around. You were educated in the American school system. You don't want to understand *why* things are the way they are, you just want to know *how to make money*.

It's time for you to put numbers to work. Let us, then, enter the world of *corporate* accounting, where minor tweaks can lead to millions. These tricks are used by the accountants and check writers in every industry, but business cheaters use them best. Note: This chapter provides just a few numerical ideas for "making crap up," but there are many, many more. The only limits are your imagination and your desire to Get Rich Cheating.

## Earnings Per Share

This is the figure that's just asking for it. The key to accounting cheats: earnings per share. "The Number," as it's known on Wall Street.* It's the distilled bottom-line, cold, hard figure of how much your company makes. It's so easy, just one number, sitting there, waiting for you to play with it. Manipulate it like your parents manipulated you. If The Number beats expectations, not only do you get your earnings bonus, but your stock price will rise and you will get doubly rich. If you do so by cheating, you'll get that extra satisfaction of following in the golden footsteps of the Great Cheaters.

Facing pressure to increase The Number—from their investors, directors, ex-wives, and bookies—some mediocre cheaters pursued aggressive business tactics like the Soviet Union's** five-year plans: short-term superficial gains, built on shaky foundations, destined for failure, but intimidating, scary, and making a few people very rich and powerful.†

Sure, you can actually "earn" more—lower costs, increase productivity, have a good product, et cetera—but that seems to take thought, effort, and understanding. What about maneuvers that don't require business knowledge or callused hands?

---

* Alex Berenson, *The Number.* There really are a lot of great ideas in this guy's book, which explains how many of the Great Cheaters did their thing.
** You remember the Soviet Union, right? You'd better, because it's coming back, although this time it's going to be called "China."
† Berenson.

# Get Rich Cheating

*"Over the long run, all the accounting and financial tricks in the world can't turn a failing business into a success . . .* But they can in the short run. *And sometimes, with enough tricks, the short run can last a long time, long enough for executives to make tens or even hundreds of millions of dollars selling stock whose value has been inflated by pumped up earnings."** 

The short run's all you care about when you Get Rich Cheating.**

Companies have always lied about their earnings.† Financial reports are full of digits, columns, headings, words, and pictures. There are a lot of companies out there. No one's going to look through all the details of each report. That's why The Number is so important: Because people don't want to do all the math. Just make it whatever you want. What's a stray penny here or there? Nothing. Ask Gus Gorman from

---

\*   Berenson. Emphasis added.

\*\*   In the mid-eighties, companies stopped paying cash dividends, which allowed earnings per share to remain fictional: If you never had to pay out what you claimed you earned, how could anyone know if you could actually do so? In the nineties, tax laws encouraged companies to shift to performance-based pay. This awesome combo—fictional earnings and earnings-based pay—led to quick riches for a few, which led to "quirky" accounting in pursuit of quick riches for the many. *Sigh . . . those were the days.*

†   From 1997 to 2000, the S&P 500 companies collectively told the public that their profit grew by 40 percent, but the figures they submitted to the federal government showed that profits actually *fell* by 10 percent in that period (Berenson, p. 210—this guy's good). This may have been partly an attempt to stick it to the tax man but was certainly a fun way to stick it to the money man too.

*Superman III.** A penny a share on ten billion shares is a mere $100 million. No one will ever notice.

It's called "fudging the numbers," because it's the hot, gooey, chocolaty topping that holds together our sundae of deception.

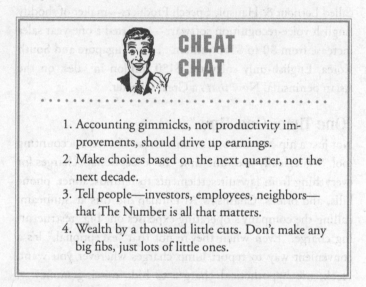

**CHEAT CHAT**

1. Accounting gimmicks, not productivity improvements, should drive up earnings.
2. Make choices based on the next quarter, not the next decade.
3. Tell people—investors, employees, neighbors—that The Number is all that matters.
4. Wealth by a thousand little cuts. Don't make any big fibs, just lots of little ones.

Frankly, there's no such thing as an exact earnings figure. These are just approximations, best guesses. All companies must make assumptions since they're using speculative numbers for everything from sales to pension growth to deprecia-

---

\* Gorman, played by Richard Pryor, made at least $85,789.90 by creating an algorithm that took the fractions of every penny from each employee in Lex Luthor's company and . . . Oh, cripes, I'm not going to explain everything. Google it.

tion of assets to a bunch of other important-sounding items. With so many assumptions, even honest companies—don't laugh, there may be some—make mistakes. *You're not honest, are you?*

Just say you sold a bunch of stuff. *Just say it.* A company called Lernout & Hauspie Speech Products—maker of shoddy English voice-recognition software—reported a one-year sales increase from $0 to $150 million . . . in Singapore and South Korea. English-only software, $150 million in sales, on the Asian peninsula. Now *that's* a Great Cheater.

## "One Time, One Time"

Not just a hip-hop intro, it's also a Great Cheater's accounting tool. Strategically use "one-time" or "exceptional" charges for everything from lawsuit settlements to refunds, toner, phone bills, and bribes. Chainsaw Al Dunlap did this at Sunbeam, calling the company's operating expenses one big "restructuring charge." Even when they're not that "exceptional," it's a convenient way to report lump charges wherever you want. Heck, use hypothetical charges to hide missing money. *A Martian Attack Defense Fund?* Sounds exceptional to me.

## A Girlfriend in Canada

Foreign corporations using international accounting standards are no longer required to adjust their financial statements to comply with U.S. accounting rules, meaning that it's okay for things to get lost in translation.* *Nice!* So just be foreign and announce, "One brown coconut = $7 million. Invest in me!" Or . . . report losses on U.S. investments, but claim massive gains on overseas investments that—*oh no!*—the U.S. authorities can't verify because of international law. Fairfax Financial Holdings did this neat little trick. Trust them, they've got lawyers.

## B.F.F.

Make fake deals with friendly companies, swapping overvalued assets in a way that allows both sides to book a profit on the trade. This was one of the great innovations of Enron's Andrew Fastow, using "special-purpose entities" with ingenious names like JEDI, Chewco, and Raptor to move expenses off of Enron's books and create phony profits. It also retroactively inspired a series of Steven Spielberg and George Lucas films.

In 2007, the SEC came down on Veritas Software for a deal it made with AOL back in 2000 because *both* companies reported $20 million in revenue from a license and advertising swap. *Picky, picky, picky.* Leave them alone to make their money, SEC.

---

* *Lost in Translation* is also the name of the movie that gave pre-collagen Scarlett Johansson her big break. *Coincidence?*

## More Time Traveling

Enron brilliantly booked future contracts as current earnings, even though it had no idea what those contracts would be worth, whether they'd actually get paid for them, or if they'd even actually exist. The company called this accounting method "Mark to Market," which was shorter than the original name, "Whatever we want to pretend to earn at some undetermined date in the future." Penn Traffic allegedly inflated income by prematurely recognizing promotional allowances like payment for inclusion in supermarket circulars. *Yes, Virginia, there is massive corporate fraud in the Daily Shopper.*

If the future's not your thing, don't be afraid to go backward in time. Rebook the sales you've already reported. No reason you can't count a single transaction over and over and over again. That's what footnotes are for.* For years, Computer Associates would immediately book sales on acquisitions, even though they weren't going to be paid for a long time. This gave CA huge earnings. When money actually began to come in from these transactions, CA couldn't book that income because they already had . . . *unless* . . . they changed the way they did accounting. So they did, counting payments for old transactions as new income, even though they'd already accounted for them earlier. *Computer Associates got paid for the same thing twice!* Simply put: Awesome. I dare you, friend, to cheat better.

---

\* Duh.

## Change Your Number

Make one set of numbers via GAAP and another however you want. Tell investors, "Trust me. I'm a . . . [whatever you are]." Many companies use EBITDA (earnings before interest, taxes, depreciation, and amortization). What about EBIT-DAM (EBITDA plus M for marketing costs)? Or my favorite: EBBS (earnings before b.s.). Computer Associates switched accounting methods in the middle of its run to glory,* so why shouldn't you?

## Overstate Estimated Pension Returns

Lucent and hundreds of other companies did this. (Old friend Mr. Pension isn't just for robbing employees.) Claim you've invested wisely and report high earnings. Ignore the fact that you're really using the money to build a condo for Mrs. Featherbottom, the admissions officer at the nearby boarding school. Your stock portfolio will skyrocket and your kid will get a decent place to discover recreational drugs.

## Improper Vendor Chargebacks

A chargeback occurs when a store asks a vendor for a refund because the customer returned an item. Or, as in the case of Home Depot, a chargeback occurs whenever you want it to. The company artificially inflated the cost of returned mer-

---

* In January 2001, CA's own numbers claimed a $247 million profit, while the GAAP numbers showed a *loss* of $342 million. Now *that* is Get Rich Cheating we can all be proud of.

chandise in order to increase chargebacks. One store boldly charged vendors for four times more glass than it actually sold. This clever practice provided Home Depot "a material portion of its revenues and profits"* and it used its power position to prevent vendors from complaining or withholding payment. While all this may seem "wrong," here's a question: "How big was CEO Nardelli's severance, again?" *Mmm-hmmm.*

## Split Your Company . . .

. . . into a bunch of smaller ones, a la Tyco, in order to allow each to use smaller one-time charges and other methods to tweak earnings. Wealth by a thousand cuts.

## Subsidiaries

(a) Put all your losses on their books, and (b) pass them money that they return to you and you, in turn, classify as "profits." The long-distance company Tel-Save shifted many of its expenses off to another public company, Group Long Distance, in order to increase its earnings.

> **Le$$on:** *You put your left foot in, you take your left foot out, you put your left foot in, and you shake it all about. You do a sham transaction with a subsidiary, that's what it's all about!*

---

* *The New York Post* (quoting the *Post* is a form of cheating too).

## Vacation Days Pay

Qwest manipulated the account of accrued employee vacation days to improve its bottom line. Perfect. Why should Qwest obey vacation pay rules when it doesn't even follow the rule of "U after Q"?

## Options for Everyone!

They're not counted as corporate expenses, your employees think they got money, and you can always just fire those employees before the options vest. *Genius!*

$ $ $

Phew, that was exhausting, but those accounting gimmicks are just the tip of another iceberg on the sea of cheat. (More ideas available with a credit card at www.afoolandhismoney aresoonparted.com.) Ultimately, when it comes to using numbers to enhance your bottom line, here's the bottom line: Make up your bottom line.

# 15

# The Basics of Competition

## Where the Invisible Hand of the Market Meets the Middle Finger of Cheating

You can grease the numbers all you want, but they only impact what's going on *inside* your world. What about the competition? Don't forget, America is a very competitive place (nothing's changed since Part I of this book). Many successful people worked hard, learned from their losses, studied their rivals, committed themselves to improving, stayed motivated, and eventually triumphed. From athletes to entertainers to executives, their stories inspire the masses. They were, however, dumb. They could've just cheated.

Our economy is based on the free market model, whereby healthy competition and free-flowing information move supply and demand into an equilibrium so every baby is happy and each puppy romps forever in a field full of squeak toys and kibble.

The truth is, babies turn into drunks who run over puppies with cars, and Great Cheaters get rich by making a mockery of fair competition.

Here are some proven techniques for crushing those who get in your way.

## Play Dirty

There are a lot of "rules" out there. Guess what? Rules were made to be cheated. Like the Great Cheaters before you, recognize rules as opportunities to fill your pockets with cash. You must walk right up to the line and then realize the line doesn't apply to you.

Play dirty. Isn't that the essence of cheating? I know you don't have time for semantics—you've got money to cheat. So trust me, it is. And if you can't beat 'em, screw 'em. Rat 'em out, drop a dime, squeal, inform, double-cross, betray, be a traitor, a Judas, a turncoat, a tattletale. Hey, nothing wrong with being a stool pigeon if your cage is lined with money.

## All's Fair in Love and Sports

The athletic fields grow some of the most inspired dirty tricks. From eye gouging to watering down baselines to corked bats, Vasoline, spitballs, goo on Kenny Rogers's hat, nail files on a curveball, throwing dirt in an opponent's face, and jabbing a hockey stick in someone's groin, every sport encourages playing dirty. Oakland cornerback Lester Hayes had thirteen interceptions in 1980, almost entirely because his body was covered in Stickum; Carl Edwards of NASCAR would take the cover off his oil tank, tweak his spoiler, or sell his mom if it'd give him a few hundredths of a second. Hey, boxing isn't even a sport—it's just a series of cheats, though I admit Mike Tyson raised playing dirty to a new level when he bit off part of Evander Holyfield's ear. *He bit off another human's body part just to win a boxing match . . .* and a few extra bucks, of course. Now *that's* commitment to cheat-cellence.

## Dirty Rotten Elected Scoundrels

Political dirty tactics have been around since Andrew Jackson called John Quincy Adams a royalist and murderer and Thomas Jefferson's opponents labeled him a French atheist who'd turn voters' daughters into mindless trollops. Yes, that may have been accurate (TJ threw some great parties at Monticello), but most political treachery isn't based in reality. A Great Cheater need not worry about such fleeting concepts as "truth."

For modern reference, look no further than Karl Rove, Rasputin to George W. Bush, who engineered the 2000, 2002, and 2004 Republican electoral victories. Cheaters of all faiths should drop to their knees and ask, "WWKRD? What Would Karl Rove Do?"

*Push polls.* In 2000, recorded messages were left for voters in South Carolina asking if they'd support John McCain if they knew he had an illegitimate black baby. "We're not saying he does, you know, but, hey, just in case." So spread rumors about your political opponents, competitors for a movie role, CFO, and investigators.

*Use the power of the attorney general* to investigate your opposition or halt an investigation of yourself. Fire those who don't comply.

*Redistrict.* Redistricting lets a Great Cheater win more elections and consolidate power to keep the appropriate people rich. Tom "The Hammer" DeLay led the redistricting efforts in order to get more Republicans in office. It was cheating . . . and *dramatic.* When he inspired Texas Republicans to gerrymander districts,* Democrats actually fled the state to deny them a quorum.** So DeLay got the Department of Homeland Security and the Federal Aviation Administration—you know, the departments designed to settle petty political disputes—to track them down like dogs. Dogs who won't let them cheat.

*Attack ads.* Swift Boat Veterans for Truth is just the most notorious one. Senator Max Cleland lost limbs in Vietnam, and Rove ran ads against him basically saying, "The Democrats are going to take your arms—and we don't necessarily mean your guns." So do one about your competition, whether political or not.

---

* Gerrymandering is a form of redistricting in which electoral district or constituency boundaries are manipulated for electoral advantage. Gerrymandering can help or hurt specific voters, like political, racial, religious, or class groups. It has nothing to do with a cartoon cat chasing a cartoon mouse.

** A quorum is such a number of the members of any body as is legally competent to transact business. Still not a cartoon cat.

# Get Rich Cheating

Scene: Night. Dark, ominous jail.

Sound effects: Slamming cell doors, screams, clanking chains.

> Voice-over (VO):
>
> *"Burger King is baaaaaaaaad."*

Burger King laughing maniacally.

> VO:
>
> *"Burger King doesn't want your
> schoolkids to live."*

Giant finger pointing at screen, then to group of children eating Whoppers and keeling over.

> VO:
>
> *"Burger King uses German recipes and French fries
> made from the tears of crippled babies."*

Grainy footage of Nazis marching, French surrendering, old lady weeping.

> VO:
>
> *"Burger King: Good for Islamic fundamentalism. Bad
> for America."*

---

Small print: Paid for by the Committee for
McDonald's Forever

Race-baiting (Willie Horton, Harold Ford Jr.), ques-
tioning sexuality, distorting records, using Photoshop to
put funny hats on opponents . . . these are just some of the
brilliant, innovative, and clever tactics that some might call
"dirty," but you should call "effective enough to keep me and/
or my colleagues in office, and ensure the favors that will lead
to riches." *Hooray!*

## Issue Threats

Threatening people is like puberty for cheaters: Putting
someone's existence at risk increases the flow of cheatosterone.
The old "You'll never work in this town again!" gambit isn't
enough. Today's Great Cheater needs to walk into someone's
store and mumble, "Nice place. It'd be a shame if anything
untoward were to happen to it." Call Vito and Tony to lend a
hand. Maybe show up flipping a quarter under a streetlamp in
a fedora. Ask, "Your wife . . . how is she?"

How could you use threats to get rich? Good question.
Good answers:

- In the 2008 Democratic primaries, Hillary Clinton's
  surrogates threatened the DNC, Nancy Pelosi, and
  others over their support and interpretation of rules.
  These were her allies! Hey, she was just showing she

knows how to govern. *Had she threatened a little more effectively, she could've gotten elected and then gotten richer.*

- Anthony Pellicano—good guy to Hollywood's elites— was accused of threatening reporters who might damage stars' earning power with (a) pulling alongside a reporter's car, pointing a gun at him, saying "stop," and then "bang!" (so he knows how to pantomime—big deal); and (b) putting a bullet hole, a fish, and a rose in a reporter's car (she was a woman, so the rose was a touch of class).

- Amgen might've cleverly told small clinics that if they switched to less expensive treatments, the drug company would impose much higher fees that would cripple their operations.

- In real estate, buy up buildings with rent-controlled apartments, fabricate claims of unpaid rent or illegal sublets, sue, sue, sue, and let the power of your attorneys crush your tenants' will to live. Once they leave, put in some chrome furnishings, call it "modern luxury," and sell it to a confused, hairy guy from Long Island for thrice the price.

- Use economies of scale (i.e., you're big, they're small), market positioning, and monopoly status to undersell local operations and drive the competition out of business. When you are the sole remaining vendor, enslave the population in your dungeons. (*See* Walmart, most major motion picture studios, Starbucks.)

- Kill the competition. Literally (*See* Soprano, Tony) or figuratively (*See* car, electric).

Basically, when it comes to threats, just act like the mob. *Question*: Ever wonder why mobsters walk around in sweat suits even though they have hot women and boatloads of money? *Answer*: Are you talking to me? I know you ain't talking to me.

**Le$$on:** *"Bada bing!"* —Bada Boom

# Wealth Through Redefinition

When confronted with a restriction that he doesn't like, the Great Cheater finds wiggle room with semantics.

- In 2007, 103 MLB players claimed the therapeutic-use exemption for attention deficit disorder so as to keep using Adderall, amphetamines, and other drugs. This was an almost four-fold rise from the number claiming the exemption in 2006.* *Why the change?* (a) Stricter testing, (b) brilliant and daring redefinition of "attention deficit disorder," "therapeutic use," and "I'll give you $50,000 to say I'm exempt, Doc," and (c) "Shut up and pitch, man—I'm totally tweaking!"
- Jose Canseco redefined "pages" and "words" by using a six-hundred-point font to get his latest grunting opus, *Vindicated*, up to 260 pages.

---

* Michael S. Schmidt, "Increase in Drug Exemptions Leads to Change in Rule," *The New York Times,* January 19, 2008.

- The Spanish basketball team at the 2000 Sydney Para-
  lympics won the gold medal. Ten of the twelve members of the team had no disability, mental or physical.
  They simply redefined mental deficiency to mean "lack
  of gold medal."

## Ideas for Stealing Ideas©™®

Here's one way to Get Rich Cheating that will *blow your
mind*: intellectual property. The Law of Ideas. *Ideas!* Weird,
isn't it? In law school, I was fascinated by intellectual property
law. I figured it would impress or confuse some undergrads
enough to sleep with me. Boy, was I wrong. Chicks do not dig
dorks with body odor and a little bit of knowledge. My bitterness and frustration became a hatred of intellectual property
rules that clouded my vision . . . until the Great Cheaters
showed me the way.

In the last fifteen years, intellectual property law has
evolved so quickly—with the internet, wireless technology,
globalization, bad pop music—that it's hard for the law to
keep up. In other words, it's ripe for the picking.

There are the basic scams: patent infringement (Aqua-
man stealing fish-communication technology from a Maine
lobsterman); copyright infringement (often called "piracy" or
"bootlegging" after Blackbeard, who was caught smuggling
Billy Joel CDs in his wooden leg); trademark infringement
(this book should be printed in the shape of Nike's swoosh);
and employee raiding (hiring employees of a competitor to

find out what they know). Basic stuff you too can learn while wasting three years in law school.

## CHEAT CHAT

Intellectual property laws confer rights—trademark, copyright, patent, et cetera—for a particular form in which ideas are expressed or manifested. Basically, if you own the idea for something, you own all the moola that comes from doing something with that idea. Turn it into a book, musical, movie, lunch box, or SpongeBob bicycle chain.

## California Cheating

The creative professions are where the most exciting idea theft takes place. Disgruntled losers who did *not* make jillions have accused others of script theft for everything from *Heroes* and *Grindhouse* to *Pirates of the Caribbean*, *The Matrix*, *Rounders*, *Broken Flowers*, and *The Crybabies Who Weren't Smart Enough to Make Millions Before Great Cheaters Swooped In and Cleaned Up*. Led Zeppelin allegedly stole lyrics and tunes from unknown blues artists, Avril Lavigne and Miley Cyrus from untalented hacks. Comedians Carlos Mencia, Jay Mohr, and Denis Leary are among those accused of joke theft. And I'm pretty sure *Star Wars* was a rip-off of my 1976 diary entry, "Today I learned to scream like a giant wooly space warrior." *I want my royalties.*

Mark Zuckerberg probably stole the idea for Facebook from Harvard classmates and then made a gagillion, men with lisps and feather boas copy and resell fashion designs (as do big companies like Gap), and even Cindy McCain "borrowed" recipes and passed them off as her own to help her husband's campaign. Your local drugstore has "knockoff," "generic," or "copied to make money" versions of Tylenol (nonaspirin pain reliever), Listerine (lister-flavored mouth wash), and Q-Tips (stick these in your hearing-hole); every successful TV show or movie spawns a series of copycats (all of which are really just rehashing *Hamlet*); and even Timothy Goeglein, President Bush's top liaison to religious groups, stole material from a column for a published essay. The devout one must've asked himself, "WWJD?" *Answer: He'd cheat.*

Don't be afraid to steal ideas in the ethically regulated field of journalism too. With the crumbling of newspapers and traditional media, it's hard to make a decent living as a reporter. Some can't even afford to live in the city they cover, *but* you *can* make it big if you become a superstar selling books, bagging babes, and ruffling feathers. So why not join the likes of Stephen Ambrose and Mike Barnicle and just borrow someone else's work and pass it off as your own? Then when controversy follows, so too will book deals and speaker fees. Hey, we can't all be Tucker Carlson, getting story ideas transmitted to him through his bow tie.

## Spies Like Us

Sometimes you have to go cloak and dagger. Great Cheaters don't just nip the ideas of their coworkers, bosses, and competitors; they tap their phones, steal their signs, monitor their transmissions, and take all of it to the bank.

Our own government put at least $43.5 billion in the 2007–08 budget to spy on us, just to make sure we're not plotting anything that might threaten their wealth-producing schemes. In 1972, Richard Nixon was so paranoid about his political opponents that he had his henchmen spy on Democratic headquarters. He even spied on himself, recording all his Oval Office conversations. The scandal, named "Watergate" after the hotel where the spying took place, brought down the president and launched ten thousand totally inappropriate uses of the suffix "-gate." Lazy pundits owe their livelihood to Nixon. Just slapping on "gate" when you can't think of something original is a form of getting paid for cheating too.

Corporate espionage is big business. Here are some prime cheating examples:

- In 2006, IBM and Cisco Systems announced plans to provide a wireless network for all of Silicon Valley. You mean two tech companies will control a system that connects to every computer in the tech center of the world? *Hmmm, I wonder where they'll get all their future ideas?*

- A secretary working at Coca-Cola plotted to steal secrets about new products and sell them to Pepsi. Sure, Pepsi ratted her out and now she's on trial under the Corporate Espionage Act (boo!), but we know that's probably only because what she found out wasn't very profitable. *Make sure your spies get good stuff!*

- Apple used the name "iPhone" for a new product even though that name was owned by Cisco. They didn't wait around for a "court" to "rule." They just took it! (Cisco also claims to own the rights to "The Thong Song.")

The New England Patriots are probably the greatest sports team ever assembled. They got that way by videotaping opposing offensive and defensive signals in order to gain an advantage. The discovery and overblown reaction to their activities became known as "Spygate," because, well, see above. The Patriots' problem was their method of spying, which was prohibited, not the spying itself. So, clearly, it's still okay to spy in sports (and I'm sure the Patriots have figured out how to do it better already).

The NFL commissioner basically admitted that everyone's been spying since the dawn of time: "I'm not sure that there is a coach in the league that doesn't expect that their signals are being intercepted."* That's why they cover their mouths when they talk. It's not halitosis (well, it was for Mike Shanahan, but not for anyone else). Everyone's doing it!

- Weeb Ewbank of the Baltimore Colts was so convinced the Giants were spying, he pantomimed his pregame speeches. He believed he was being spied on because he spied on others.
- Tom Landry admitted to intercepting opponents' radio signals.**
- The Oakland Raiders have always pretended to be worthy of greatness ("Commitment to Excellence"), but their claims fall short because their alleged spying—via a helicopter over a New York Jets practice—was too weak to win. Who can determine tackle stances from five thousand feet in the air? More like Commitment to Not Trying Hard Enough.

Baseball players routinely peer in to see catcher signals, and the stealing of signs has become so prominent in that game that most third-base coaches flail about like Baryshnikov on crystal meth. (You should really see his *Cocaine Swan Lake*.) Lip readers, hidden microphones, drunks with binoculars . . . sports teams have always found ways to steal signals.

---

* John Branch, "In the N.F.L., It's Not Cheating Until You Start Videotaping," *The New York Times,* February 17, 2008.
** Mark Bowden, "Sacks, Lies and Videotape," *The New York Times,* May 18, 2008.

# Get Rich Cheating

Here's an original Get Rich Cheating suggestion: Go to a graveyard. Dig up the most recent, richest corpse. Cut out its brain. Bring the brain to your castle and put it inside the hollow head of the monster you've created from discarded body parts and old tin cans. Wait for a storm. Use lightning and evil to bring your creation to life. Give it a soul. When the villagers attack with pitchforks and torches, sneak into their homes and steal their plans for the next computer operating system. You should also own the only pitchfork and torch store in town to jack up the prices. (*See* ExxonMobil, Paris Hilton, NY Yankees, et al.)

## Lawyers Are a Good Idea (Really)

If you can't beat 'em, sue 'em. Use the courts to file frivolous lawsuits over intellectual property rights. Lawyers are expensive—trust me, I'm a lawyer—and most companies will simply pay you a nice big settlement rather than going through the cost of litigation.

Such was the case when NTP sued BlackBerry maker Research in Motion and Treo maker Palm for patent infringement of the handheld device technology. Ever heard of an NTP handheld? Me neither, but the company's making money without doing anything but filing legal paperwork.

Similarly, Great Cheater Jonathan Taplin has perfected the intellectual property sour grapes lawsuit. In January 2007, he sued Apple, Google, and Napster, claiming they're all infringing upon a 2005 patent that covers commercial internet distribution of audio and video. Back in 2002, he sued Movielink about another undeveloped idea. Next thing you know, he'll claim to have invented pants.

Didn't *you* invent pants too?

Look, why do the hard work of coming up with brilliant ideas and concepts when you can just rip 'em off? In this age of easily accessed information, I can only think of a few original thoughts to sum up my feelings on the subject: It's the best of times, it's the worst of times. Show me the money. It's hard out here on a pimp. And, of course, who let the dogs out?

# 16

## Collusion Is Fun

### For Everyone!

Competition is cool. "Rah rah" and all that crap. But what if you don't want to compete? What if, instead of beating each other up, you got together with your fellow cheaters to take advantage of the everyday saps toiling in the lower 99 percent?

Great Cheaters don't care about competitors, as long as they're not blocking their own money-making schemes.* Great Cheaters are so narcissistic, they often don't even know there *is* competition. Why? Because genuine competition is for regular, honest folk—not you. Getting rich is your main objective; crushing others is a secondary concern.

Our culture creates a myth that there's this great free-for-all market, but really, the big boys don't compete. They combine and manipulate, collude and exploit. Working *together*

---

* Hollinger's Conrad Black, for instance, actually cheated most of his money via newspaper noncompete clauses, i.e., specifically by *not* competing.

can lead to riches for all. Collusion, monopolies, oligopolies, cartels. If you're the only ones providing a good or service, you control supply and can create demand, excessively overcharge, and make a bundle.

## Work with Your "Team"

Power companies, cable providers, baseball owners, OPEC. Archer Daniels Midland scammed the international lysine market and gained millions. Sure, some execs went to prison and the company got the highest antitrust fine in U.S. history and was ordered to pay a $400 million class-action settlement, but, man, it had good times.

Hollywood studios formed the AMPTP (Alliance of Millionaires Prepared to Trounce Peons) in order to make the annoying writers, actors, and directors accept about 1.3 cents for every $10 billion the studios make. There's been price-fixing between Sotheby's and Christie's; the five largest *elevator* makers were in cahoots in 2007.* Exxon and Mobil are the same company, Maytag and Whirlpool share the same bored repairman, and you tell me the difference between Coke and Pepsi, Burger King and McDonald's, Visa and MasterCard, Bert and Ernie. You can't tell me the difference. There's no difference. They're all closeted puppets.** You should be one too.

What about throwing games for cash? Wonder why every

---

\*  Going up? Profits are.
\*\*  I'm sorry, that's just the last two. The rest are inspirational companies that feign competition to profit from the modern consumer instinct to believe in the market.

sporting event has official betting lines? Why the Vegas odds are so prominently displayed, even though gambling is illegal in most of the country? It's so you can Get Rich Cheating. Gambling and sports: the two great cheats that cheat great together.

- Denny McClain and Pete Rose both excelled at baseball,* and both helped spread the wealth to themselves and others by maintaining ties to gamblers and mobsters. Might it have helped that they had a vast impact on the outcome of games? *Um . . . yeah.*
- Nikolay Davydenko, the world's number four tennis player, retired from a match against number eighty-seven, but not until enough money had been bet against Davydenko to make his retirement a double entendre among the double faults.**
- The 1919 Chicago White Sox—a.k.a. the Black Sox, a.k.a. made more money in a week than they had in five years—got together to throw the World Series so they could be remembered in the John Cusack vehicle *Eight Men Out.*
- There has never been a clean, honest, nonfixed boxing match in the history of the sport. *Ever.*
- Athletes routinely engage in point-shaving, a trick by

---

* McClain was the last pitcher to win thirty games, Rose is the all-time hits leader, and both are kinda dumbasses, which is why they were caught.

** Davydenko was cleared "on a technicality" (see Chapter 27), a cheating maneuver akin to, say, "pulling a hamstring" in a tennis match.

which they take the razor of their abilities and trim the final score down to the stubble of rich.

Thank you, gambling industry! You make me and a bunch of guys named Tony very happy.

It's not just the point spread that creates sports cheating. Professional teams often get together and "talk" about what to pay their players—or what not to pay them, in the case of 2008's unemployed Barry Bonds. Keep salaries down, keep caviar and mistresses up. Several leagues have instituted rules against tampering and collusion, even as they themselves engaged in it (I'm *praising* you, National Pastime). I'm sure a clever cheat like you can manage to organize a phone tree among a few executives.

## Bribe Yourself Some Friends

Find someone who has something that will help you "win." Give them money, promise them money if you succeed, or show them a videotape of them taking your money and threaten to broadcast it. Prepare your victory speech.

Jack Abramoff made millions arranging bribes of politicians at the highest levels. His clever bribery included not just money, but meals, sports arena skyboxes, and trips to Scotland, Russia, and the exotic Mariana Islands for sun, golf, and—in Russia—vodka-induced viewings of Sarah Palin's house. Sure, his schemes eventually brought down White House officials like Steven Griles and David Safavian, Repre-

sentatives Bob Ney and Tom DeLay, and other aides, lobbyists, and himself, but he got a lot done along the way.

> **Le$$on:** *DeLay's nickname, "The Hammer," prob-
> ably comes from his love of the cash-hiding capacity
> of parachute pants, popularized by rap sensation MC
> Hammer.*

Everybody wins with bribery—unless, like Blagojevich,
they never get the cash. Representative Randall "Duke" Cunningham received at least $2.4 million to do the good work
of Great Cheaters. Not a bad take for a guy with a lame nickname. Ever the organized one, Cunningham even kept a led-
ger to tabulate the bribe-to-benefit ratio for each conspirator.*
Note: Such record-keeping might be efficient, but it's probably
the first thing you should burn when the Feds close in.

I'm sure you'd heard of Cunningham, DeLay, and
Abramoff, but were you aware that lesser-known Great
Cheater Richard Scrushy donated $500,000 to Alabama
governor Don Siegelman in exchange for a position on a
state governing board? Or that CVS executives John Kramer
and Carlos Ortiz were accused of paying Rhode Island state
senator John Celona to influence legislation? Or that William
Jefferson (D-LA) probably hid his bribe money in a freezer
Jeffrey Dahmer–style? You didn't know? *Now you do.*

The Great Cheaters own the officials who score, judge,
and verify all their deeds. Sometimes literally.

---

* Really.

Somebody got rich when Olympic judges cheated titles from the 1972 U.S. basketball team, 1988 boxer Roy Jones, 2002 ice skaters Salé and Pelletier, and that cute little girl who lip-synched at the Beijing Olympics in 2008. *Awwwww.*

Have you seen the NBA lately? Every play involves violence. A referee could call a foul at any time, affecting the game, the final score, individual statistics, contract negotiations, campus activities, the spread of unwed mothers, and what shoes get what kids killed where. Tim Donaghy was forced out of the NBA after the FBI reported that he bet on games he officiated and made calls affecting the point spread. He passed along information about who was refereeing games, relationships with players, players' physical conditions, et cetera to gambling friends. He'd get paid for his help. He'd get rich, and they'd get rich. It was a win-win no matter who won-won. Donaghy and others didn't just rig NBA games for gambling money; they also did it so that the league could benefit by having a longer playoff series with more revenue, stars who never fouled out, and exciting controversy to keep people talking—and buying league publications—long after it became less reputable than professional wrestling. *Get yourself a friend like that.*

Donaghy was dumb enough to get caught, but there are more officials out there, all willing to take a *little* money to help the cheating player, owner, or gambler make a *lot*.

Offer kickbacks, a percentage payment given to someone with the power to make a deal happen, i.e., an after-the-fact bribe. It's like paying cabdrivers in Jamaica to steer people to your discotheque. *Hey mon, you letting me take care of dat.* Lawyers at Milberg Weiss paid kickbacks to plaintiffs to help file suit against corrupt companies and get big fees. The firm paid $11 million in more than 150 class-action suits, which earned them $216 million. Spend 11 to make 216. That's a great cheating ratio!

Did financial aid officers inappropriately steer college students to Student Loan Xpress just because they were in cahoots? I'm not saying they did and I'm not saying they didn't, but I'm definitely not not saying you shouldn't do the same thing.

*And don't forget foreign countries!* I'm not talking Europe, with their "affordable" health care and socialized "arts funding." I'm talking about places where no one in his right mind wants to go—start with the third world, but soon skip straight to the fifth or sixth world (mmmm, Bulgastainistan). Find poor countries with rampant corruption, tons of natural resources, and currency worth less than the paper on which you print your invoices. All you have to do is drill, ship, and cash in.

Take Chevron, which might've made at least $25 million in profits from a scheme of kickback payments to Iraq in '01 and '02 under the UN Oil-for-Food program. Please note, aspiring cheat: "Oil-for-Food" is a nice-sounding scheme. Kickbacks are a kind of food . . . they feed your wallet.

If you feel bad about duping war victims, don't go to the doctor. Ninety-five percent of the joint-maker industry paid over $300 million in fines (just a fraction of what they made) for funneling bribes through fake consulting agreements to get doctors to use their products. In other words, when doctors make decisions about which device to insert into a patient, that decision is based upon the highest bid, not the best medicine. Good for money, not good for joints.

Medtronics allegedly arranged kickbacks for spine surgeons. Not only do the kickbacks provide financial incentive, but attempting to actually kick one's own back causes spinal injury. It's a self-fulfilling cycle of pain, cheating, and riches.

Tenet Healthcare and Medco Health Solutions are among the jillions of other companies who could've taken part in medical bribery, and among the sad few who were "caught."* They exchanged kickbacks with doctors, health plans, or drug companies, and they did so because America has the best health care system in the world. (You can't see it, but I'm winking at you right now.)

## Rig the System

Vote early, vote often, vote from your grave. There's perhaps no purer, more American form of collusion than vote manipulation. Great Cheaters have controlled the levers of power by pulling the levers *for* power ever since cavemen fought to rule the clan and engaged in literal mudslinging.

---

* Tenet and Medco, along with Chevron and Medtronics, all wisely deny any wrongdoing, like all Great Cheaters should (see Chapter 28).

**Succes$tory:** *"Thog not true Neanderthal. Him part Homo sapien. Not fit to lead fire circle!"*

—Adlai Stevenson*

Stuffed ballot boxes, lost ballot boxes, vote suppression, voting multiple times, preventing opponents from voting by claiming they're felons or breaking their machines or not liking their skin color. Democracy is America's gift to the world. It's what the Founding Fathers fought for: making sure every land-owning white man had the right to keep getting rich.

Chicago Mayor Richard J. Daley and Boss Tweed are just two of the hundreds of "machine" politicians who used patronage, pressure, and local precinct captains to drum up, marshall, fabricate, falsify, and pull out of their arse votes to keep power and support national leaders who might, say, possibly, send a few million dollars in road money their way.

American elections are run by people who have a stake in the outcome, a horse in the race, a future employer they'd like to impress. Where else could a presidential election be decided by a Supreme Court full of justices appointed by your father, in a state where your brother is governor and your campaign chief is secretary of state? Nowhere else. Why? Because if it happened anywhere else, we'd invade and install a legitimate regime.

But wait! Thanks to technology, Great Cheaters' system-rigging opportunities have only expanded since 2000.

---

* No, not really.

## Collusion Is Fun

The new way to Get Elected Cheating: electronic voting machines. They don't have reliable paper trails, they often switch, subtract, or undercount votes, and they're "run" by elderly women who can't program a VCR, let alone operate a left-turn signal. Constantly proven tamperable and less reliable than an ATM, electronic voting machines are gifts to the technically inclined who carry around magnets and computer code. You know who should have magnets and code? Your "campaign consultant" Vinny.

He who counts the votes usually wins and always enjoys the process. Senator Chuck Hagel worked for the voting machine company that counted votes in his Senate runs, and Diebold Voting Systems' CEO said in 2004 that he would help "Ohio deliver its electoral votes" to Bush,* so you too should hire, bribe, or become a voting machine company.** It's what our Founding Fathers wanted. (See Article XXXIV, "Congress shall make no law abridging the right of land-owning white men with poufy wigs to steal elections.")

America: Land of Cheatportunity.

---

* Clive Thompson, "Can You Count On These Machines?" *The New York Times Magazine*, January 6, 2008.
** The 2002 Help America Vote Act authorized $3.9 billion for new technology buys. So, sell them new technology, like the "from which office would you like to cheat me some money?" computer coffee machine iPod commemorative desk calendar.

## 17

## Take Me to Your Uncle

### Oh Say, Can You Cheat?

Besides accomplices, enablers, numbers, and the competition, there's one more person with whom you can Get Rich Cheating. Your uncle. No, not the one with the whiskey breath and the grabby hands—the other one. With the red, white, and blue goatee. Sam! Your Uncle Sam! It's easy and fun. The Great Cheaters use the government to make money, change rules, stay out of trouble, and beat less-connected rivals.

The Great Cheater thrives where others fail. *Check that*: The Great Cheater thrives *because* others fail . . . at doing even the simplest of tasks. By "others," I mostly mean everyone related to your uncle, i.e., the United States government.

Yes, other industries have exploitable incompetence—you can always get an easy "win" by taking on retarded organizations like NBC Television, the New York Knicks, or the Democratic Party—but the government is a special breed of screwup whose cheating potential can't be underestimated. There is easy money to be had. Don't let poor people get it first.

# Government Not-Know-How

Look, young cheater, people who work in government are tired, fat, sleepy, and unshowered. They just want to sit back and collect paychecks. They don't want to rock the boat or even *row* the boat: They just want to lie down in the boat as it bobs on the sea of bureaucracy. They won't notice your submarine plucking treasure off the ocean floor.

*Remember that pesky Hurricane Katrina?* Because of government failure to fulfill its most basic duty—protecting its citizens—there was plenty of post-water opportunity for the clever contractor, con man, and life-raft operator: fake insurance claims and charities, falsified housing requests, overpriced trailers, tarps, and water, misspent government aid, and unverified $2,000 debit cards spent on guns, porn, and booze. Heck, the insurance companies even got rich off the government failure in Katrina, basically throwing up their hands and saying, "We're not paying for this mess . . . but thanks for your premiums, which, by the way, have to go up . . . so we can, um, uh, pay for this mess. *Gimme!*"

**Le$$on:** *Don't just chase ambulances. Chase the National Guard.*

*Remember when government regulators inhibited your activities?* Me neither. In recent years, Big Brother has installed industry-friendly officials at all the agencies overseeing the nation's workplaces, food suppliers, toys, product safety, and more. The FDA failed to follow its own policy for inspection of imported Chinese goods, like the blood thinner Heparin and various tainted toys. So? It only caused brain damage and death, *not loss of profit.* Despite product recalls, in early 2008, the chief of the Consumer Product Safety Commission actually opposed getting a bigger budget and staff. Yes, in coming years people will probably act like they're more open to regulation—what with the liberal media shoving all these dead babies, autistic teenagers, and choking toddlers down our throats—but it won't amount to anything substantial. So go on and sell your shady products; you won't get caught, and though a penny saved is just a penny earned, a corner cut can earn you about $10 million.

## Entitlement Programs Have Your Money

Government entitlements are a prime source of cheatable money, with Medicare the Great Cheaters' favorite. Who's gonna deny Grandma treatment, even if Grandma doesn't exist? *No one.* Who's gonna know Neurontin has encouraged doctors to ignore less expensive alternatives? *Same no one.* Who's gonna pay for it? *Medicare.* Among those that have been caught overbilling, claiming excessive rebates, getting hospitals to increase demand for their products, or simply submitting false claims are Medco, Tenet Healthcare, Omnicare,

SmithKline Beecham, and Medtronics.* Those are just the ones dumb enough to get caught: Imagine how many Great Cheaters are out there scamming this program.

Medicare's the most popular entitlement to exploit, but there are others, like Social Security, child support, welfare, and, of course, worker's comp, a.k.a. "Oooh, my arm! I think it's broken."**

Part of what makes these programs so cheatable is the bureaucracy behind them. Ahh, bureaucracy. There's no more beautiful word to a cheater, except maybe "not guilty." Ever talked to your right hand and realized it had no idea what your left hand was doing? Well, that's what the government is like, except both hands are usually giving you money. Rely on it to do inexplicably awesome and incompetent things for you, without even asking. For instance:

- In 2008, Attorney General Michael Mukasey suspended the Los Angeles U.S. attorney's public corruption office. Why? Because it was investigating public corruption, and that just wouldn't do.
- Congress pays billions in subsidies to get people to use ethanol as an alternate source of fuel while at the same time supporting tariffs and quotas that guarantee we'll

---

\* Having read an early draft of this book, these fine companies also deny any wrong-doing. *$mart move.*

\*\* Quote from *Caddyshack*. Example from Arkansas State Senator Nick Wilson, who led a group of ten people, which diverted $5 million in state money from programs including child support and legal aid. He diversified his cheating portfolio. You should too.

use less. You may not have known that, but the ethanol people did, and they're tickled green. Money green.

- The Labor Department provided Walmart with advance notice of "surprise" labor inspections.

- In 1993, a new law required corporations to pay taxes on compensation over $1 million. It was intended to dampen executive pay (*ha!*) but it actually made companies shift to performance-based incentives, whereby the better the corporate earnings, the higher the pay. Thus Chapters 9 (Fir$t Things Fir$t) and 14 (Hire the Numbers) gained their awesome cheating power.

- Due to an "oopsie" in regulations, the oil and gas industry pumped gas from federal lands without paying about $7 billion in royalties. Attempts to recover the money were dropped because the Department of the Interior didn't want to put resources into an "unwinnable war." (Insert your own ironic oil-and-unwinnable-war comparison.)

- A federal judge ruled that government cannot even *change* the drilling incentives that provided those billions. Once you get the incompetent train rolling, it's hard to stop. *Toot, toot!*

- Campaigns, with millions in small donations and high turnover, are easy targets. Candidates of all parties are routine victims of embezzlements of $100,000 or more by wise cheaters.* Just mismanage, siphon, bleed, suck

---

* Leslie Wayne, "Awash in Contributions, Campaigns Offer Tempting Targets for Thieves," *The New York Times*, May 27, 2008.

them dry. Christopher Ward of the National Republican Congressional Committee saw $360 million pass through his hands—well, not all of it made it all the way through his hands. A lot stuck to his hands and had to be wiped off inside his pockets. Must've been using Lester Hayes's Stickum.

- The Bush Administration started pumping millions of dollars into faith-based initiatives, which required neither testing nor quantitative results. So, Great Cheaters, just become pious and create a faith-based initiative, like some group for sick kids or crippled kittens. What's your faith? The almighty dollar.

## "Only Little People Pay Taxes"*

Ah, taxes. A special brand of government incompetence. Trillions of Americans cheat on their taxes. It's true-ish! From creating phony transactions and fake losses to taking advantage of the kindhearted ineptness of the IRS, Great Cheaters know that the country's money is theirs to keep.

## Excessive Expenses

Basic tax law: You're taxed on your profits, so *to pay no taxes, make sure you have no profit.* Profit is income minus expenses. So have lots of "expenses" to cancel out income and, *voilà,* you'll owe no tax.

---

\* Leona Helmsley.

**Le$$on:** *This whole "having no profit" thing is just for the tax man. For shareholders, fans, and easily fooled aspiring actresses in Hollywood clubs, you're always making billions. Just make sure ne'er the two shall meet. Since 1990, the profits reported to share-holders of the largest U.S. companies have been about 50 percent higher than those reported to the IRS.*

You can deduct ordinary and necessary expenses. Great Cheaters love terms that are open to interpretation. "Ordinary and necessary." I'd say that includes just about everything from office supplies to private jets, self-paid consultant fees, Jacuzzis, Cialis, and pills for male pattern baldness. You don't really have to have these expenses. Just say you do and pocket the truth.

**In$piration:** *"They just wrote down numbers on pa-per and claimed losses. It was just like fantasy baseball, except the taxes not paid for were real."*

—Senator Carl Levin (D-MI)*

What have the Great Cheaters taught us about expenses?

- Tyco's Kozlowski had the most fun ever deducting that birthday party for his soon-to-be-ex wife. With clients

---

* About the Quellos Group, a tax shelter boutique based in Seattle. David Cay Johnston, "Tax Cheats Called Out of Control," *The New York Times*, August 1, 2006.

mingling among the Roman gladiators and an ice sculpture of David that released vodka out of his hoo-hah, he could write off the urethra-infused Grey Goose, et cetera.

- Okay, maybe the Jeffries Group's deduction for strippers and "dwarf tossing" at a bachelor party was fun too.
- Send profits to overseas subsidiaries and call them investment "expenses." Enron (*all hail the king!*) had almost nine hundred offshore subsidiaries for this purpose. I believe their U.S. tax liability was around twelve bucks.
- Major motion picture studios routinely overstate their expenses to get hundreds of millions in tax incentives from states like Louisiana and Michigan because those places desperately need the occasional thin, pretty person.
- About 600,000 federal contractors owe $7.7 billion in back taxes.* Most of them are defense contractors. Who's going to make them pay? The government, with its body-armor-less army? *Ain't gonna happen.*
- Boeing considered taking a tax deduction for a $615 million settlement over . . . wait for it . . . *ethics* charges. They didn't. Chumps. *You wouldn't pass up that chance for ironic savings, would you?*

---

* "Tracking the Spoils of the Private Sector," *The New York Times,* April 27, 2008.

# Delaware and Bermuda

Your company is from one of these places. Really, it is. *It is.* Multinationals use overseas shelters to lower payments by at least $50 billion per year.*

Bermuda has no income tax, which saved Tyco about $400 million. There are more than 16,000 foreign companies "based in" Bermuda, as opposed to about 2,500 that actually do business there. (Bermuda law actually *prevents* some of them from carrying on local business.) Bear Stearns and insurance companies are particularly skilled at avoiding billions in taxes via Bermuda.

Delaware? *Oh boy.* Great Cheaters know the state basically exists to serve corporate America. About two-thirds of the Fortune 500 companies are incorporated there, and rules are friendly regarding insider deals, compensation, and protecting executives from liability. In 1963, a law was even rewritten to make it state policy "to maintain a favorable business climate and to encourage corporations to make Delaware their bitch." Wait, sorry, that last word should be "domicile."

The Delaware courts love inspiring executives too. In 2006, a U.S. bankruptcy judge came out against things like disclosing executive pay because it might create "low morale and an unhealthy work environment." *How amazing is that?* He's worried that if the peons know they're getting screwed by us, they'll be upset. Thanks for the cover, Delaware legal system!

Look, you don't actually have to be in one of these places.

---

* The Brookings Institute.

We all know Delaware's such a cultural vacuum that the FAA reroutes planes to avoid its airspace. Just set up a P.O. box in Wilmington. As for Bermuda, same thing, but go visit now and then. Nice beaches, fairly hurricane-free, and you deserve a fruity cocktail.

## What Income Tax?

Now that you have extra change in your pocket—hopefully on the order of millions, if not billions—you're probably worried about paying personal income taxes. Don't. I'm not just here to help you Get Rich Cheating, but also to *Stay* Rich Cheating. Luckily, so is Uncle Sam.

We've all heard how tax cuts disproportionately benefit the wealthiest Americans and the share of income going to the top 1 percent of Americans continues to grow, while that going to the other 99 percent falls, et cetera, et cetera, et cetera, blah, blah, blah, good, good news all around.* But do you know just how much they really want us to stay rich? If you knew, you'd take action! *Oh wait, you are. You're reading this book.*

Regard:

- Audits of *low*-income Americans are on the rise and millions had their meager refunds withheld within the last five years. Not only does this prevent people from climbing the economic ladder, but all this poverty and unfairness helps create great blues music.

---

* Outraged politicians have demanded that the 1 percent expand to at least 1.5 percent.

# Get Rich Cheating

- On the flip side, the Bush administration laid off tons of IRS agents responsible for tax enforcement on us wealthy folks.
- Studies by people who clearly need other things to do have also shown that the IRS has spent less time auditing the nation's largest corporations over the last five years, despite the recent scandals, and agents are pressured to complete them faster with less scrutiny.
- If those rushed audits do find any unpaid taxes, the IRS is using private debt collectors, who are not only inefficient (getting only about 8 percent of our hard-hidden money) but probably related to your Brooklyn friends Vito and Tony.

All this, even though we super-rich deprive the IRS of $70 billion per year—that's seven cents on the dollar of "honest taxpayers," a.k.a. "losers."

Normally, tax cuts mean less tax cheats. But not now. According to an IRS study, in 2001 alone, tax cheats shortchanged the American government by $345 billion—an amount equal to 75 percent of the 2008 budget deficit. That's a lot of money and a lot of cheaters. And you know what? *They can't catch us all.*

So start lying on those personal tax returns. If tax evasion can be a common bond between Wesley Snipes and Willie Nelson, it can bond you too. So do it. *Do it now!* Remember, you can't spell "making millions by cheating on your taxes" without "cheating on your taxes."

# Ask Your Uncle for a Do-Over

## Get Him Drunk First

Don't like the results of your competition? Miscalculated your cheating? Got careless with your "honest errors"? Well, simply ask for a do-over—like when you were in third grade—and let government-endorsed methods enrich you again.

## Bailouts

Having trouble with your business? Bankrupt because of poor management, embezzlement, and irresponsible speculation? Well, just ask your pals in office to bail you out, subsidize you, and protect you. Bear Stearns got a huge government bailout despite being at fault for—and briefly enriched by—their failures; the auto industry should've been taken out back and shot but instead got billions; airlines did it after 9/11 even though their business model was already going down; Northrop Grumman asked for $200 million to help recover from Hurricane Katrina; Long-Term Capital rode the "bail us out because we're so big" train; at least 40 percent of ADM's agricultural profits are from heavily subsidized or protected items that cost U.S. suckers, er, consumers, millions of dollars; and the U.S. steel industry's only products these days are requests for protective tariffs.

Breaks are given to those companies because they're part of a "special industry." So join a "special industry" with unique hardships and needs: airlines, cars, corn, bad business. Hire tons of people you can't afford to pay and for whom you don't have any work; then rescuing you will become a matter of national concern. It's for the stability of international markets and world peace, the community, employees, and public morale. Politicians don't want to incite panic, especially among the poor people who vote for them at home. (More on bailouts in Chapter 26: The Financial Crisis.)

> **In$piration:** *"Rescuing failing companies obviously runs the risk of creating moral hazard—if we insulate people from the consequences of their irresponsibility, they're more likely to be irresponsible in the future."*[*]

That's a risk you should be willing to cheat.

## Restate This!

Okay, you've made millions, right? Just by manipulating some numbers with creative accounting tricks. But you can't lie forever. *I know!* I can hardly believe I'm saying it myself, but it's

---

[*]    James Surowiecki, "Too Dumb to Fail," *The New Yorker*, March 31, 2008.

true. Don't worry, America makes it easy. Once you've lied in financial statements and filings for a while, just restate them.

"Restatement of earnings." Come on, everyone's doing it, some more than once. Freddie Mac has restated so often that it might be the company's core competency. It's all the rage. According to the SEC, there were 3 restatements in 1981, 49 in 1997, over 1,000 in 2002, over 1,200 in 2006, and 8 trillion since noon today. Ten percent of the companies listed on U.S. exchanges re-filed statements in 2006 after finding errors.* One in ten! It's not a "lifestyle choice"—they were born that way.

Restatements have gotten bigger too. From 1997 to 2002, the average market value of restatements quadrupled from $500 million to $2 billion. Fannie Mae's restatements from 2001 to 2004 alone equal $6.3 billion. Just pick up today's business section and I guarantee some company has restated an amount worth more than God.**

What does a restatement allow the Great Cheater to do? After making gobs of money for falsified performance, you just say, "Whoops." It's a legitimate way to beat the system. It's so simple. Imagine:

```
"I earned $500 million this year. Invest in me!"
           Flash forward two years.
"I'd like to restate my 2005 earnings by about
$500 million. Thanks for the boost in stock price!
I cashed out big time! P.S. Please bail me out."
```

---

\* According to the research firm Glass Lewis.
\*\* Not a guarantee.

There's no catch. Nothing illegal or immoral, though it's certainly fun. Frankly, you can restate anything. Cablevision might want to issue a restatement because the Knicks are not "world champions forever and ever." They actually "stink."

A restatement isn't even a slap on the wrist. It's a pointing of the wrist toward an Excel spreadsheet and a fitting of that wrist for a diamond bracelet made of cheat. It's the ultimate do-over. Don't you wish we could restate other things in life without consequence? Like when you told the doctor to give you the prostate exam or honestly answered the question "Does this make me look fat?" or said you "did not have sex with that woman." Don't you wish you could restate *those* moments? You can't, but you *can* restate the lies that get you the money to buy your way out of all that trouble.

*Isn't that cool?* So fake, fake, fake . . . and restate! Especially once you've cashed out and gotten far, far away.

# Chapter 11 Is the Best Chapter in Any Book

If all else fails, declare bankruptcy, grab your severance, and let everyone else fight it out. It's that simple. Really. Bankruptcy allows your deliberate and destructive misdeeds to be forgiven and to be done all over again. Along with its cousin restate, bankrupt is a Great Cheater's best—and most legitimate—friend.

## Bankruptcy What?

Bankruptcy has the dual purpose of allowing a debtor—
one who has debt, such as you—to make a fresh start, while
his or her creditors—those to whom the debt is owed, or
"chumps"—are repaid as best as possible. Isn't that cute? Pay
back people you've scammed! *Ha! As if!*

Bankruptcy is not a crime. *Not a crime.* There's nothing
wrong with declaring bankruptcy, which means it's one of the
safest—if least exciting—schemes in this book. Bankruptcy
fraud, now that's a legal no-no, but, hey, we're not defrauding
anyone, right? Riiiiight? *Wink.*

## Bankruptcy When?

Bankruptcy dates back to biblical times. Even Genghis Khan
had a rule that mandated death for anyone who thrice became
bankrupt. (Another reason to avoid living in the time of
Genghis.)*

Lately, bankruptcy has regained popularity. Over 80 percent of the largest U.S. corporate bankruptcies have occurred
since the year 2000.**

---

\* The Time of Genghis was actually the name of my high school band.
\*\* Oh, but no, this scam isn't affected by the Bankruptcy Abuse Prevention and
Consumer Protection Act of 2005. *That* law only affects individuals, not corporations.
I mean, come on, like they'd pass a law to hurt us? No, that was a change pushed by
banks and lenders to make it harder on regular folk to declare bankruptcy. That way
they can't avoid giving us the money *we* need to create schemes that accrue debts to
those who then squeeze the regular folk again for more money. It's the circle of life . . .
which furnishes a lot of Italian villas for the Great Cheaters.

## Bankruptcy How?

Modern *corporate* bankruptcy can fall under either Chapter 7 or Chapter 11.

In Chapter 7, a company goes out of existence and debts are often repaid by submitting assets for resale and distribution. That's one way to go.

In Chapter 11 bankruptcy, your company attempts to stay in business while a court supervises "reorganization" of the company. Oh, but glory be, during reorganization you are protected from your creditors. In other words, the people you owe can't do anything—not lawsuits, collections, garnishing wages, nor shaking fists—to get their money back. That's right, the courts give you protection against the very people you've screwed over. *Protection from the consequences of your incompetence!* You'll still get your salary, your severance, your performance bonuses and more. It's easy: Just file some paperwork . . . Heck, hire someone to file paperwork, and when they submit an invoice . . . *Whoops! You're bankrupt!* In the words of Yakov Smirnoff, "What a country!"

At one point in 2006, over half the airline industry was operating under Chapter 11. They freed up cash, stopped making debt payments, even had price wars . . . all with court approval, while pilots and flight attendants got fired and your Tumi tote ended up in Ottawa.

In Chapter 11, you have to create a plan for reorganization ("steal more money" is a good plan), and get your decisions approved by a bankruptcy judge. Another quick question: Who was a major contributor to that bankruptcy judge's campaign? *You?* Oh, really? Gosh, hope he approves your decisions.

### Bankruptcy Why?

Some commie pundits claim that operating under Chapter 11 protection provides an unfair advantage to the bankrupt company, that the system provides an "escape hatch" to incompetent management. Yes, it does excuse incompetent management . . . Shouldn't it excuse *corrupt* management too?

### Bankruptcy Who?

The bigger the company, the more devastating the consequences of bankruptcy—to investors, employees, and debtors. Notice who's not on that list? You!

# Rematches

These are not technically government do-overs, but rematches are wealth-generating do-overs sponsored by a "governing body," so . . . get to it. There are approximately 73 million divisions of boxing and about 22 gajillion title fights, each garnering about $72 blaxamillion in income for promoters, networks, and combatants. So after every "legitimate title fight," demand a rematch. If not for the glory of the chintzy belt, then for all the little starving children in Africa who *need* you to make $50 million over the course of fifteen three-minute rounds. *That's forty-five minutes of work!* Think of the children.

# 19

## Friends, Cheaters, Countrymen

### Lend Me Your Uncle's Ear

Government incompetence provides plenty of opportunity to cheat, but what if you don't want to rely upon Uncle Sam's stupidity? What if you'd rather just work *with* him to guarantee your fortune? That's a great idea, but in order to do so, you must get to know your Uncle. *Intimately.* So make a connection, because government connections will get you the ear of government, and, as any preschooler knows, the ear bone is connected to the money bone.

How have the Great Cheaters gained access to government?

## Campaign-Donate to 'Em

Politicians need to be reelected, and they need money to do so because whoever has the most money wins elections. (Votes and issues? *Whatever.*) You have money. Give some to them and they'll put you in a position to get more. Start hanging out at political events, law schools, and fund-raising dinners. Also, always vote against term limits.

The 2004 presidential election saw the candidates spend $440 million, a figure that was eclipsed in the 2008 campaign way back in April. In 2008, candidates, interest groups, and political parties spent a record $5.2 *billion* on national races.*
All that money wasn't raised by kids selling their bicycles or donating five bucks online. There's a lot at stake in these elections, and a lot of opportunity to get rich, stay rich, and cheat rich.

The biggest campaign contributors often come from old-timey, mom-and-pop industries like banking, energy, real estate, telecom, tobacco, and pharmaceuticals. Most cheaters support Republicans, but you, aspiring cheat, should hedge your bets and donate to both parties, i.e., also the Democrats (shudder).** Enron was a huge contributor to George W. Bush's campaign but actually gave to both parties. If you're strapped for cash, target your donations to candidates who work on committees you need to influence or before which you're likely to testify.

## Lobby 'Em

The most cheatable legal form of government influence is lobbying. Named after the art of soft-tossing a ball in the air

---

* Jeanne Cummings, "2008 Campaign Costliest in U.S. History," Politico.com. http://www.politico.com/news/stories/1108/15283.html.

** Other parties don't count. No other parties: not Green, nor Libertarian, nor Vegetarian, nor Dominatrix. *No other parties.*

for an inept athlete to smash, lobbying is a multibillion-dollar industry. It doesn't matter who's in office—lobbyists are on the prowl.

Who has lobbyists? All the old-timey mom-and-pops from above. If *they're* worth listening to, so are you . . . unless you're poor. We never hear about lobbyists for the poor because they don't *have* a lobby, they *sleep in* a lobby. *Bwaa-ha-ha-ha-haaaa.* Even Native American tribes have lobbyists. You'd think they would've learned not to deal with the government after the whole "give us Manhattan and we'll give you beads and smallpox" thing, but no. . . .

What do lobbyists do? They are the conduit of information between the companies they represent and the People—or at least the people who represent the People. It's how Alaskan congressmen get the idea for a $200 million bridge from a tiny village to nowhere and how OSHA is reminded to loosen mining regulations since there haven't been any mining problems in years. (*Cough, cough. 'Scuse me, that's just my miner's lung.*) Lobbyists used to work just to prevent harmful legislation, but now, with starting salaries around $300,000 and about 50 percent of former elected officials returning to D.C. as lobbyists, they've gotten proactive in the pro-business, pro-lobby, pro-cheating environment.

It's democracy in action. How else could you explain congressmen who pass laws preventing the government from negotiating prices on prescription drugs right before they work as lobbyists for those drug companies?* Or how the head of the Justice Department's environmental division buys a million-dollar home with the lobbyist for ConocoPhillips, then nine months later lets the company delay installing equipment and paying fines?** Or the $150,000 departing payment to Michael Baroody, nominee to lead the Consumer Product Safety Commission (CPSC), from his former employer, the lobbying arm of the National Association of Manufacturers, members of whom are—or, rather, *were*—the CPSC's targets? Or the fact that there are approximately fourteen kajillion lobbyists for every congressperson in Washington and it's a $2.8 billion industry? That's about $17 million per day for every day that Congress is in session,† which is when elected officials audition for these high-paying lobbying jobs while representing the poor, less-cheating people? There's a revolving door between lobbyists and government officials. It's the type of door our Founding Fathers would have installed had the technology existed, and they would've spent less time flying kites in the rain.

Your lobbying role model is old friend Jack Abramoff. His reach spread viruslike throughout the halls of power from the White House (he personally lobbied the Bush administration hundreds of times and arranged tons of such meetings for others) to the office of congressional aides to Tom DeLay and

---

* Oh, Billy Tauzin (R-LA and CEO of PhRMA), you minx!

** The official, Sue Ellen Woodbridge, was cleared of any ethics violations because it's obviously the way to be.

† "It's So Much Nicer on K Street," *The New York Times*, June 6, 2008.

the like. He scored victories for a wide variety of clients, from small island countries to fake grassroots campaigns, Tyco, and Native American tribes.* He was the best at "encouraging" officials to vote *against* limits on internet gambling and immigration, stronger labor laws, more taxes on casinos and corporations, ending sex sweatshops, IMF bailouts, and the criminalization of taking candy from babies.

Yeah, there are some new lobbying rules, but, really, as expected, they're full of loopholes like allowing last-minute proposals to be inserted out of public view. Loophole or awesome-hole? *You decide!*

## Fly 'Em Around

Candidates and congressmen need private jets because they live in states that are far, far away from Washington, D.C. There isn't a politician in the world who wants to travel with the masses after weeks of spilling Veuve Clicquot all over his nine-hundred-thread-count sheets and tallest mistress, a.k.a. "legislating." Unfortunately, their salaries only allow them to fly coach, and most aren't married to beer distribution millionairesses. So give them a lift! Think of your plane trip as patriotically sparing a hard-working American from the din of the common folk and the need to explain why he's buried in the cleavage of his "assistant."

---

* Another fair trade: The Native Americans give us their land and heritage; we give them gambling, alcoholism, and Jack Abramoff.

# Build 'Em a Home

Say you know a senator who's dealing with rules regarding your business. Well, why not offer him some renovations on his home like VECO Corporation? Senator Ted Stevens got hundreds of thousands of dollars of free work from the company of oil-services honcho Bill Allen, and, golly gee, back in D.C., Stevens pushed for big government projects that benefited Allen. *Nice.*

Not much of a builder? Then just buy 'em a home. The defense contractor Mitchell Wade bought Duke Cunningham's home for $1.675 million, even though it was worth less than $1 million, and lo and behold, soon got tens of millions in government contracts. *What a coincidence!*

# Help 'Em Out

During Vladimir Putin's first term in office, Gazprom, a Siberian gas field and energy company, bought the only opposition media in Russia, NTV. That certainly endeared Putin to Gazprom's cause: The Kremlin pressured the oil giant BP to sell its stake in Gazprom for way below its value. President Putin later met with executives from Shell and BP on other deals, such as renaming Red Square "Gazprom Is Totally Awesome Square."

# Bring 'Em on Board

Putting former politicians on the board of directors very subtly suggests to current ones that you'll do the same for them. Annette Nazareth left the SEC to join the private sector. As to where she ended up, check her recent ruling, the "Any Company Hiring Annette Nazareth Is Immune from the Law" decision, and work backward. Former governor Jeb Bush was appointed to the board of Tenet Healthcare in April 2007, just three months after he left office (nice restraint). Russian president Dmitry Medvedev, who was chairman of Gazprom's board, replaced Putin, who became Russia's prime minister, replacing Viktor Zubkov, who became—*wait for it*—chairman of Gazprom! At one point, former U.S. representative William Gray was on nine boards, former senator Sam Nunn's been on about seven, and former Senate leader George Mitchell is a director at approximately all of the companies in the world.

## Give 'Em a Name

Senator Henry Jackson was a Democrat from Washington State who earned the nickname "Senator from Boeing" because of his unabashed support of the aerospace company employing his voting base.* The nickname "Scoop" comes from the action necessary to lift the bales of cash from taxpayers' pockets onto Boeing jets.

## Give 'Em a Stake

Former FDA commissioner Lester M. Crawford owned stock in companies that just happened to be in need of FDA ap-

---

* Robert Scheer, *The Pornography of Power* (New York: Twelve Publishing, 2008).

provals. Who gave him that stock? Great Cheaters. Edwin Foulke, a choice to head the Occupational Safety and Health Administration (OSHA, or, as it is known in Canada, "oh, sure"), previously worked as a lawyer protecting companies from—*wait for it*—safety and health liability.

## Get 'Em Laid

What goes best with power and money? A nice pinot? A twenty-four-hour news channel? Nope. Sex. Former Newark mayor Sharpe James sold city properties below value to a "companion" who had well-defined "assets" and who then resold the houses for a "huge profit." Oil company employees gave paid vacations and consulting fees to—and, of course, did crazy drugs and had illicit sex with*—thirteen officials from the Department of the Interior. All they got in return was billions in business. If you don't want to "do the dirty work" yourself, remember that today's horny politician can't be too careful when hiring prostitutes, right, Spitzer, Vitter, and Tobias? *Oh my!* So form a discreet service for the discerning lawman and offer some complimentary "consultation" for the right "legislation."

---

\* The reason everyone's always having "illicit sex" is that the word "illicit" actually makes "sex" sound sexier. It's too tempting. Might as well be "naughty sex" or "sex worth a spanking" or "ha-cha-cha . . . sex." You want to stop illicit sex? Call it "eating oatmeal with Grandma."

# Be One of 'Em

Dick Cheney is your hero, but he's not the only politician u$ing his power wi$ely. From the likes of Representative Rick Renzi, who may have financed his reelection campaign by selling fraudulent insurance policies and forced constituents to buy land from a secret business partner; to President George W. Bush, whose patriotic fear-wrangling led the nation into a war that enriched his buddies; to Rod Blagojevich, demanding money and appointments for a Senate seat; to Sarah Palin, with her expensive stylists and plush family—politicians are the kings and queens of abusing the public trust. What about the political *bureaucrats* entrusted with the execution of the government's programs? They're executing their vacation plans, raiding the Treasury, falsifying welfare and Medicare claims, sucking city pensions dry, selling tax and personal information to the highest bidder, and generally being very, very rich.

*But they've sworn to serve the people!* Golly gee, Mr. Gullible, what happens if they don't maintain that oath? Does the book they swore upon hit them in the head? *Nope.* So no worries, go to town . . . Rich Town . . . located just outside Washington, D.C.

## 20

Get Rich Cheating

# The Scam from U.N.C.L.E.

## I Want You! To Get His Money

Once you have government connections and influence, you must use them—and abuse them. Now that you've convinced Uncle Sam to let you do whatever you want, it's time to start doing whatever you want. These hard-earned contacts may only last until the next election, so get cheating.

Even George Bush knew about the fleeting nature of government hookups. He sucked every last penny he could out of his presidency, passing last-minute energy, environmental, and financial rules that benefited his buddies, even as a nation obsessed with campaign '08 forgot he existed. If he can use the government to get rich, can the rest of us? Yes We Can.

## "Win" Government Contracts

Government contacts will get you government contracts. In the alternate universe of $400 hammers, a government contract is a fountain of gold that never stops flowing. Good buddy Halliburton is the king of government deals, often no-bid and high-pay. They've had about $18 billion in contract work in Iraq alone. How did they do it? Well, it probably helps that their former CEO is "your hero." Even if you're not that lucky, connections all along the contract process can help direct the work your way.

- Former Housing Secretary Alphonso Jackson steered hundreds of thousands to friends for work in post-Katrina New Orleans and the Virgin Islands. Um, it's called vacation planning.
- Ninety percent of the Small Business Administration's budget in high-unemployment areas went to VBP Group, an Arizona company with zippo small business experience. The company was run by former Bush Agriculture appointee Vernon Parker. He got the contracts just four months after forming the group, even though it normally takes two years to get certified by the SBA, let alone receive money.
- Moving Water Industries Corp. recently won a $32 million New Orleans drainage contract from the Army Corps of Engineers. The company's bid matched up nicely with the specifications of the Army's request for bids, which just happened to have been taken verbatim, typos and all, from the catalog of . . . *ding!* . . . Moving Water Industries Corp. Hey, it's not their fault the Army can't afford to hire competent employees.
- New York State claims that investment firms paid friends and relatives of comptroller Alan Hevesi cash

money in exchange for getting a pension management contract. And you thought a "comptroller" was what came with a Nintendo Wii.

## No Bid, No Problem

The really accomplished Great Cheaters can get their government contracts without even trying, through a process called no-bid. Spending on contracts awarded without "full and open" competition has tripled since 2000—and that doesn't include the '08 bailout. That's a lotta cash to be cheated. Former Attorney General John Ashcroft got an eighteen-month, $52 million no-bid contract simply to monitor a legal settlement between the government and an Indiana medical supplier. No public notice, no bidding—the Justice Department just gave it to him.

The no-bid process is designed for speed and limits the ability of government crybabies to put up safeguards to prevent waste and fraud. Hey, they don't have to worry. You're not going to *waste* any of the money you *fraud* your way into.

## The Best Defen$e Is a Good Offense

You know who's making nice money off the government? Honeywell, General Dynamics, United Technologies, and all the nicest defense contractors. The State Department spent about $4 billion per year on private security and law enforcement agencies alone from 2003 to 2007. The Coast Guard hired Lockheed Martin and Northrop Grumman to supervise a $17 billion modernization project. Sorta. DynCorp International got $1.1 billion to train police in Afghanistan. Well, they got their money, but there's no trained police force. Hey, they say they're on the job, so let's just take their word for it. Defense contracting: Good work if you can shoot it.

**In$piration:** *"Defense procurement has disintegrated into an incestuous relationship between the military, politicians, and contractors."* —Walter Braswell[*]

Our armed services don't like paperwork; they like blowing things up. Michael Cantrell, a mid-level Defense Department guy, extracted $350 million from the Pentagon *for projects it didn't want and for services he never provided* just by gaming the system. Army officials didn't want to get in budget fights with Cantrell's Senate friends like Trent Lott, so they just gave him contracts with no scrutiny. It was easier that way. Incest is best.

Best of all, most of these war-related contracts are . . . *drumroll, please* . . . NO-BID!

*"Even before the first shots were fired in Iraq, the Pentagon had secretly awarded Halliburton subsidiary Kellogg Brown & Root a two-year, no-bid contract to put out oil well fires and to handle other unspecified duties involving war damage to the country's petroleum industry. It is worth up to $7 billion."[**]*

---

[*] Eric Lipton, "Insider's Projects Drained Missile-Defense Millions," *The New York Times,* October 11, 2008.
[**] Charlie Cray, "No Bid and No Problem," TomPaine.com. http://www.tompaine .com/articles/no_bid_and_no_problem.php. There was more planning for the rebuilding contracts than for the rebuilding itself. Nice!

Companies like Bechtel, Halliburton, KBR, and Crest have connections to the government cash dispensers. Neil Bush—yes, another of the President's brothers—helped get contracts for his friends. (The kind of friends who paid him about $60,000, i.e., good friends.) Shocking, I know. *Cheating, you should.*

Some hippies claim that the Iraq war has resulted in the "largest case of war profiteering in history." Well, you have to account for inflation, liberal media. I mean, in 2008 dollars, the Peloponnesian War in 431 BC would have been, well, absurd.

> *"A BBC investigation estimates that around $23bn (£11.75bn) may have been lost, stolen or just not properly accounted for in Iraq . . . To date, no major US contractor faces trial for fraud or mismanagement in Iraq."\**

There's a multibillion-dollar Development Fund for Iraq paid for by oil revenue just begging for you to exploit it. Great Cheaters are reselling old equipment or submitting invoices for millions in salary without any documentation whatsoever . . . and getting it!\*\*

I mean, come on, young cheater, do I have to spell it out for you? People are literally dying for you to get rich. You owe it to them to make sure their sacrifice is not in vain.

---

\*    Jane Corbin, "BBC uncovers lost Iraq billions," BBCNews.com. http://news.bbc.co.uk/2/hi/7444083.stm.

\*\*    James Glanz, "Iraq Spending Ignored Rules, Pentagon Says," *The New York Times,* May 23, 2008.

## CHEAT CHAT
### Paid for Services Not Rendered

Charge Uncle Sam for work you've already done, you've done poorly, or you never intend to do. Meaningless-ness has its price. Michael Cantrell got money for firms to test and design things they'd already tested and de-signed, prisons and detention centers are routinely built for way below their fee, and where did the money for that Bridge to Nowhere go? Nowhere, a.k.a. someone's bank account.

Or just flat out overbill, baby. Do an hour of work, charge for a week. With all that bureaucracy, they'll never catch on. Okay, Schering-Plough agreed to a $435 mil-lion settlement for overcharges and Halliburton's always getting "cited" for excessive costs and Harry Sargeant III was accused of making $14 million by overcharging the Pentagon for fuel deliveries, but that's just because some low-level pencil pushers don't realize how much it costs to maintain a squad of highly trained junior executives to suck up to you at the snap of a finger.

## Earmarks

Earmarks are an exciting way for your government con-nections to get you money. What's an "earmark"? A tiny birthmark in the shape of a dollar sign on the ear of a giant who smashes others' dreams. Despite grandstanding reform and veto pledges by the likes of several-million-in-earmarks-getting candidate John McCain, the spending bill for fiscal year 2008 included more than 2,200 earmarks worth $1 billion,* and that number is sure to increase because that's what Thomas Jefferson would've wanted.

Not all the cash for these earmarks even makes it to where it's ostensibly supposed to go.** Money gets lost along the pipeline. *Why?* Because Great Cheaters like you punch holes in the pipeline to siphon off barrels of sweet, sweet cash.

Those numbers are probably not accurate, because tracking the billions in earmarks is not-accidentally difficult to do. *Whatever.* There's a lot of earmark money: Yes, there was a new ethics rule in 2007 about earmarks and pork barrel spending,† but that just made it more difficult to *request* money. Methinks congressional staffers can figure out how.

## Rules, Schmules

On the off chance that you can't get around the rules, bend 'em, twist 'em, and change 'em. Legalize your schemes for cheating success.

---

\* Ted Stevens got the most ($94.1 million) because Alaska has so many needy caribou.

\*\* Ron Nixon, "Not All Earmarks Are Paid in Full, and a Senator Wants to Know Why," *The New York Times,* May 20, 2008.

† "Pork barrel spending" is using a pig to lure monkeys out of a barrel in order to fill that barrel with ill-gotten booty. Less fun, but more rich.

**In$piration:** *"If you set the rules . . . it's almost impossible to lose."* —Karl Rove*

After *repeatedly losing* the state, the Republican Party tried to change the rules of the electoral college so that California's votes in the presidential election would be distributed proportionally, not winner-take-all. Haven't succeeded yet, but give 'em time. (Maybe they'll bag that and just change the rules to allow an Ahnold to be president.)

After—and during—*repeated losing*, Hillary Clinton tried to change the rules regarding the counting of delegates in Michigan, Florida, and Texas during the '08 Democratic primaries. All those states have strong college football traditions, i.e., a high tolerance for cheating. *Coincidence? Probably.*

Speaking of football, after *repeatedly losing* to the New England Patriots in the playoffs, the Indianapolis Colts whined their way into meeting with the rules committee to change the game. Peyton Manning benefited from the NFL's subsequent greater emphasis on the illegal contact rule. He set records, won a championship, and made millions for himself, his team, and whoever produces the ten thousand commercials he's in every goddamn day.

Let the Great Cheaters lead by example:

- GWB got installed as president when the Supreme Court decided to change its rules on federalism and

---

* Karl Rove, "How to Win in a Knife Fight," *Newsweek*, April 7, 2008.

equal protection, but just for that case, not for future decisions. It's a "Get out of not being president for free" card.

- W., just like every president, signed a zillion "midnight regulations" to give away what little government money was left without that annoying "I'm Just a Bill" song from *Schoolhouse Rock*.

- The administrator of the EPA reversed a ruling allowing California to limit auto emissions after pressure from the White House. Well, duh, by the time the mutations kick in, we'll all be long gone. Let California's grandkids deal with the radioactive three-headed toads.

- As his company neared catastrophe, Angelo Mozilo of Countrywide Financial changed the company's rules to allow himself to sell hundreds of millions in stock.

- During the height of the lending boom, the Office of the Comptroller of the Currency (OCC, not to be confused with OPP) invoked an obscure 1863 law to preempt all state predatory banking laws. No reason you can't time travel to keep cheating.

- The SEC voted against allowing investors to nominate their own board members, meaning folks getting screwed by us bigwigs can still do nothing about it.

- Many states have adopted strict voter ID laws again. According to a judge in Indiana, his state's law is a "not-too-thinly-veiled attempt to discourage election-day

turnout by certain folks believed to skew Democratic."*
*Nonsense.* If you can't correctly answer the simple,
straightforward question "Are you a Republican?" you
shouldn't get to vote.

* Missouri claims their voting ID laws exist to stop illegal immigrants from interrupting the voting process.
Sure, because there's nothing illegal immigrants like
more than to go into government offices and ask to
speak to someone in charge.

## Regulations, Schmegulations

Remember when you were little and your friends came over to
play and they'd get mad because you made up the rules as you
went along because you were playing in *your* yard with *your*
toys? Well, having influence over a regulatory regime is just
like that. Only without Mom bugging you to play nice.

What's the number one thing you want to have your
regulatory regime do? Deregulate. Especially electricity. Deregulation led to Enron's profits (and the California energy
crisis, *boo-hoo*) and in Illinois it will probably generate a huge
windfall for companies like Ameren and Exelon. MBNA and
other credit card companies are huge campaign contributors.
In the past thirty years or so, they've eliminated personal
bankruptcy and had most of their questionable practices—
like hidden fees, deceptive advertising, arbitrary high penalties, and usurious rates—legalized through deregulation.

---

* Jeffrey Toobin, "Fraud Alert," *The New Yorker*, January 14, 2008.

# The Scam from U.N.C.L.E.

You can use influence over regulators in other ways:

- Ken Lay basically got to appoint all the members of Bush's Energy Task Force, and, gosh darn, didn't Enron make a boatload for a little while?
- The Big Five accounting firms—with their $39 million-ish of political donations between 1989 and 2001—successfully prevented Arthur Levitt of the SEC from changing the accounting-auditing rules, which cheated them billions.
- Why not just pass regulations that require you to get $1 million every five minutes? Why not?

The rule-making possibilities are endless: Red rover, red rover, send cheating right over. Simon says . . . cheat! No givebacks, no cooties—if I can't have shotgun then I call "cheating"!

## 21

## Misinformation Breakdown

### On the Highway to Wealth

No matter how snuggly you are with the government, you'll still need to control information to control income. Your clients, customers, competitors, teammates, voters, fans, and family must remain fools if you want them to soon part with their money. Sometimes you hide the truth, sometimes stretch it, sometimes stay silent, sometimes tell a version of the truth that will hold up in some court (of law, of public opinion, of Judge Judy), and sometimes just talk out of your rear and see what sticks.

Here are a handful of cheating ways to build a misinformation superhighway you can drive all the way to your Swiss bank account.

### Lying

*Whoa, cheater. This is a big one.* Lying is the foundation of all the cheating we've learned so far. Getting into bed with the government buys you a lot of things, but it's not going to save you from having to stretch the truth. Fudge everything, from your ability to build a hydrogen-powered car to the ads from Swift Boat Veterans for *Truth*, your earnings per share, Medicare costs, "certification," and the classes your student-athletes attend. Sometimes, young cheater, vague misstatements are too complicated. Sometimes you have to just straight-out lie.

## Politics Makes Strange Lie-Fellows

The old joke: How can you tell a politician is lying? His mouth is moving. *Oh, snap!*

Here's a follow-up: How can you tell a politician doesn't care what people who repeat stupid jokes think? He's got more money than you. *Daaaaamn, you got served!*

Politicians lie about their voting records, their intentions when elected ("Read my lips: No new taxes"), and whether or not they landed under sniper fire in Bosnia. They lie about the costs of war, tax cuts, programs, and Medicare drug benefit plans. They lie in debates, on the Senate floor, and in your face. But guess what? They're still rich. Know what else? *You* keep electing them to stay rich. Sounds like lying works to me.

George W. Bush bravely told 935 lies* leading the country into the war in Iraq, a move that has enriched oil companies, defense contractors, government subcontractors, torturers, and spin doctors. The war probably cost the American people

---

* Center for Public Integrity (CPI) study released in 2008.

$2 or $3 trillion. That money's going into someone's pocket, right? Might as well be yours.

The lies spewed during political debates constitute daring cheating because they're about people standing three feet away and often go unchallenged. Mitt Romney called McCain's immigration proposal "amnesty," John Edwards claimed he never took a dime from a lobbyist, Dick Cheney said he'd never met Edwards, and Barack Obama claimed that if Mc-Cain were elected, the solar system would be consumed in a ball of fire. None of these half-truths were corrected (though some may have proven true, right, angry sun?).

## Actor Your Age

Go on, ask people in Hollywood their age. I dare you. Then carbon-date them. They're lying. Remember *Beverly Hills 90210*, the show about high school kids? Average age of the actors playing the kids: 83.

## Miss Winfrey Would Like to Speak with You

Writing a best-selling book can earn you millions—even if it doesn't sell. All you have to do is make the story sound good enough that publishers want to buy it. Then you can work on a recommendation from Oprah Winfrey, a.k.a. Black White Oprah.

- Stephen Glass got a huge advance from Simon & Schuster to write about his "dishonest career" as a *New*

*Republic* writer. He made up a fake company with a fake website and a fake cell phone and then had a fake fifteen-year-old hack into it for a highly acclaimed investigative report. *Attention to fake detail!*

- Jayson Blair was also a lying reporter (for the *New York Times*) who got a huge book deal after being caught mid-fib. Note: Blair himself claims he got away with it because he's African American and had therefore been coddled and given breaks all his life. So, young cheater, get some minority accomplices. *Black friends: Not just for cocktail party conversation anymore!*

- Jose Canseco probably stretched his muscular truth when he claimed in his new book that Alex Rodriguez did steroids. But guess what? It generated publicity and sales for the former bash brother, who is currently using your money to buy hair gel.

- Margaret Seltzer wrote an autobiography under the name Margaret B. Jones about her life as a gang-banger in South-Central LA. Whoops, wasn't true. Not her real name, not her real ethnicity, and now she's not real sure how to spend all her money.

- James Frey—who was famously confronted by Black White Oprah—made up most of his book *A Million Little Pieces. So?* Now he's spending a million little dollars.

# Get Rich Cheating

## Don't Trust Them—They're Lawyers

Ah, law, where six minutes is a quarter of an hour. Law firms routinely overbill. Remember *The Firm*? The FDIC was overbilled $100 million and Leona Helmsley had an attorney claim to put in forty-three hours *in one day* (he's a workaholic). You might think lawyers' huge hourly fees—oh, $800 per hour—would cover office expenses. *Nope*. Wise Great Cheaters at big law firms charge clients billions for copies, trillions for secretaries, and zillions for other basic services. In one year alone, the firm of Cravath, Swain & Moore reportedly made $6.6 million from secretaries,* excuse me, "administrative cash cows." Law firms also tend to audit each other's bills, so there's little chance of being caught. (See Chapter 16: Collusion Is Fun).

## Dumb, Wealthy, and Gullible

Easily fooled rich white people are everywhere. Lie to them.

- Lululemon claimed its expensive high-end athletic wear was made from seaweed. Nope. At least the money the company cheated for its overpriced spandex was green.**
- Pets of Bel Air sold adorable puppies for upwards of $1,000 to the fab Hollywood set but didn't say they came from puppy mills—large, abusive, filthy, and crowded breeding operations. *Whatever, like totally.*

---

* David Callahan, *The Cheating Culture*, p. 36.
** Also, yes, you do look fat in that.

Young Miss Airhead will get bored with Fido and toss him soon anyway.

Go ahead, young cheater, lie. Try it. Wait a minute or two. No one said anything, right? You got away with it! Feels good, doesn't it? You know what feels even better? Another one. Then another. Then another and another and another and *uh-oh! You're rich!*

# Insider Info

A Great Cheater knows how to turn sensitive information into sensational money.

*Shows and games:* Early TV game shows like *The $64,000 Question* and *Twenty-One* were stocked with participants who got rich because of inside information, from contestants to producers, advertisers, and network execs.* After many crybabies cried, standards and guidelines changed, but not before many folks had gotten very rich cheating.

*Insider trading:* Yes, it seems very Daryl Hannah and Charlie Sheen from *Wall Street*, but it's still an option today. A *New York Times* study found suspicious or abnormal trading in 41 percent of recent mergers and buyouts. Heck, insider trading is what basically got White Oprah thrown in jail. As she'll tell you, anything she can do, you can do too. With just the items lying around your house. It's so simple.

---

\* Charles Van Doren and Herb Stempel were coached by *Twenty-One*'s producers into a scripted showdown that boosted ratings and won Van Doren some cash.

# Get Rich Cheating

Insider trading occurs when *anyone* acquires nonpublic material information and uses it to trade stocks or bonds. All inside trades, legal or not, must be reported to the SEC and most insiders have a "duty" to the corporation and shareholders before themselves. Yeah, just like I have a "duty" to come to a complete stop at every red light and report myself to the police if I don't.

The Great Cheaters see rules against insider trading as creative opportunities. Former Qwest CEO Joseph Nacchio got $52 million from illegal stock sales—*$52 million!* That's a nice day's work. One cool 2006 scam involved a clerk at *Business Week*, several strippers, and a retired Croatian seamstress. Really.*

Executives like Ken Lay, Angelo Mozilo, and their fellow old white guys secretly sold stock when only they knew their companies were collapsing. At the same time, they urged employees and investors to keep buying. They were like the captains of the Titanic telling passengers the iceberg crash was just a needed improvement in big-boat seaworthiness. Hey, no reason to incite a panic before you can get to the lifeboats— no room for women and children with all your bags of cash.

Don't forget to hide your trades! When others start buying

---

* Goldman Sachs analyst Eugene Plotkin and his friend David Pajcin used an elaborate scheme to make over $7 million in illegal, and awesome, profits. They bribed people who worked where *Business Week* was printed to get advance news of favorably mentioned stocks, then made huge purchases. In order to do so, they set up accounts in other people's names including Pajcin's aunt, Sonja Anticevic, a sixty-three-year-old retired seamstress in Croatia, and Monika Vujovic, a twenty-three-year-old New York exotic dancer. *$exy.*

to catch up, sell the stock at a higher price, then buy a year's supply of sunscreen, thongs, and those little cocktail umbrellas (oh, and rescue flares if you're going the Titanic route).

## What They Don't Know Can Enrich You

The Great Cheater embraces the Fox News Network mantra, "We report; you are dumb." In order to Get Rich Cheating, you too must exploit the ignorance of others. There are so many masters from whom to learn. A wise man once said, "Knowledge is power." A rich man added, "Shut up and gimme my skim latte already." Keep everyone in blinders. *Their* ignorance is *your* bli$$.

Agents of all sorts—entertainment, real estate, book, insurance—basically make money because they control information their clients don't have: Who's looking for an actor, where an apartment is located, how on earth they deserve 15 percent for doing nothing. That's why they—and you—hate "democratic" innovations like Craigslist. They need to keep people ignorant so their knowledge is disproportionately valuable. You should too.

Rams Home Loans relied heavily on American securities that were failing but didn't mention that in the prospectus for its IPO and made about $600 million. Duped purchasers got, technically, bubkes. *Smart.*

The Bush White House kept all its visitor logs secret so you didn't know about the plan to sell your children to Bechtel. *Smarter.*

Get Rich Cheating

A *60 Minutes* special that exposed the role of Karl Rove in the shenanigans behind the prosecution of Don Siegelman was—whoops—"accidentally" blacked out in Hunstville, Alabama, where, whoops, gosh, it all took place. *Smarterer.*

A little-noticed National Research Council panel found that changing crop production to produce more ethanol will affect water quality and availability, and the corn for ethanol might cause more damage than other forms of plants, but *shhhhhhhh*, farmers need to grow some cash. *Even more smarterer.*

The cholesterol drug Zetia, a.k.a. Vytorin, failed to benefit patients in a two-year trial ending in April 2006, but, *whoops*, Merck and Schering-Plough, who make the drug, missed their own deadlines for reporting those results. Oh pooh, now all those people will keep buying it and buying it and buying it . . . *Smarterest!*

# 22

# Public Relations

## Private Cash

If you've followed any of my recommendations, it's safe to say you've been bad, but *shhhhh, don't say a word*. What you tell the public—and how—will go a long way toward determining how rich you can cheat (and how long you remain free). You may not like to deal with "people," but "people" are your customers, investors, employees, investigators, readers, audience, and fans. You need to control what they think, feel, and believe.

## Image Is Everything

Did you know Donald Trump is a marginally successful real estate mogul who's gone through bankruptcies and business controversy? *Of course not.* You think he's a winner, a TV show host, trophy-wife gatherer, and tester of futuristic outer space hair pieces. *Why?* Because that's what he tells us he is—that's the image he self-promotes. He knows people only register the superficial stuff. If he acts like a winner all the time, we'll have no choice but to believe him, give him money to be part of the action, or get out of the way. Perception is reality for this Great Cheater. He has everyone beat before they even begin to play.

A Great Cheater distracts people from his lack of substance with attitude, presence, and style. *Look the part.* That's all you need to do. Create your own aura of success and accomplishment. Tell others you're great, and eventually they'll believe it. Make yourself an icon.

Steven Schwarzman, head of Blackstone, arrives by helicopter, even when driving's easier. "You have to make an impression. 'If you want my time, I'm so valuable, this is how I travel.' "* *You gotta flaunt it.* Gary Milby, head of MidAmerica Energy, threw a party for his daughter that was broadcast on MTV's *My Super Sweet 16.* It had horse-drawn carriages, a faux castle, and helicopters. Never mind that he'd offered investors fraudulent shares in energy partnerships and that the broadcast got regulators all over him—he looked good. And everybody wants to get with someone who looks good.

For entertainers, this has never been easier. Celebrity news is an exploding market, providing sustenance to soulless paparazzi around the world. A lot of these photographers and reporters came from families who could barely afford a Polaroid. Don't let them down. Exploit their niche. TMZ, *The Enquirer, The Insider, Crotch-Shots Weekly* . . . these enhance

---

* James B. Stewart, "The Birthday Party," *The New Yorker,* February 11, 2008.

your worth as a human commodity. Pursue them. *Bad* publicity is the best. A sex scandal? *A few million*. A sex and drug scandal? *A few million more*. A scandal with sex, drugs, and elected officials? *Priceless*.

What does Paris Hilton do again? *Nothing*. But she's making gobs of money because she's got an image, a public presence. Kim Kardashian, Carson Kressley, whoever else is on Bravo and VH1? Besides a diddle-exposing sex tape, they don't do diddly, are probably signs of an imminent apocalypse, aren't substantially adding to the world, but *are* worth jillions. They're walking, talking, rich, cheating hype machines.

Barack Obama made himself a rock star by combining hype with hope. Can't deny hope. Who doesn't like hope? No one . . . except all those who didn't think of turning it into a billion-dollar campaign—and trillion-dollar presidency— first.

Should your image even remotely reflect your actual essence? *HA!* George W. Bush campaigned as an everyman, a blue-collar schlub, even though he's really a prep-school, Ivy-educated frat boy who lived on a vacation ranch bought with oil money attained with family connections, and, more obviously, was the only one in his family with a Texas accent, even though he was born in Connecticut . . . and it got thicker the longer he lived in D.C.! It's like he graduated from Yale with a degree in Talking Like a Toothless Banjo Player.

Unless you want someone *else* to yell, "You're fired!" from beneath a helmet of hair, consider these additional cheater image-enhancing techniques:

- Get your name plastered on worthy causes. Abercrombie & Fitch got a Columbus trauma center named after it for $10 million. Sure, A&F caused the trauma by forcing kids to pursue an unattainable Aryan body image, but *shhhhh*. Nationwide Insurance named a children's hospital for $50 million, and now kids can see who's denying their health coverage right there in the hospital. *That's efficient and deceptive.*

- Pay attractive women to spend time with you. It will look like you've earned it. Chances are, if you're reading this book, you're no looker.

- Act bored. It gives you an air of authority, a presence that says nothing can faze you. *Oh, I just lost $10 million? Whatever. I don't care, ten million's not that important to me.*

- Repeat something enough times, eventually it becomes true.

- Repeat something enough times, eventually it becomes true.

- Repeat something enough times, eventually . . .

Just remember: Honesty is the best policy *only* if you do *not* want to Get Rich Cheating.

# Hypocrisy

You must walk a fine line when crafting your public persona. Sometimes, the best image for a Great Cheater isn't arrogant and successful, but humble, pious, and devout. BUT! Do not practice what you preach. For instance, John Rigas refused to allow Adelphia to carry X-rated programming, treated employees well, put his phone number on bills, and financed medical centers, all while immorally cheating his way to a fortune. Good for him. Consider these other *hypocritunties*:

- Building a million-member church based upon outrage over sexual deviancy while buying drugs and having illicit homosexual affairs. (Pastor Ted Haggard was the founder of New Life Church in Colorado and outspokenly condemned homosexual activity. He was forced to resign after being caught using drugs with a male prostitute. Cool.)

- Speaking out against gambling from Vegas. (Billy "The Book of Virtues" Bennett wrote a book called, surprisingly, *The Book of Virtues* and his Empower America organization opposed casinos. In 2003 he admitted he was a high-stakes gambler who'd lost millions in Vegas, butbutbut he only played on blackjack tables of great virtue.)

- Criticizing congressional earmarks, then requesting thousands yourself. (Bush was an outspoken opponent of congressional earmarks but has requested thousands himself. Including: $330 million to research pest control, $1.5 million for a waterway, $900,000 for an air traffic control tower in Kalamazoo—that place sucks—$12 million for a parachute repair shop, $6.5 million for asphalt research, $2 million to detect neutrinos at the South Pole, and $28 million for GE and Siemens to do go-nowhere research. What about the folks who get all this earmarked money? They're Getting Rich Cheating too, aren't they? See Chapter 19: Friends, Cheaters, Countrymen.)

- Announcing you will limit yourself to a salary of just one dollar but "forgetting" to mention your signing bonus and stocks. (Thanks for the tip, Richard Miller of Delphi! Your compensation in 2005 was $3.75 million. Your "salary" was only $1. Auto companies, take note.)

- Railing against infidelity while cheating on your spouse. (Congresspeople Henry Hyde and Helen Chenoweth, while pursuing the impeachment of Bill Clinton, were both later revealed to have been adulterers.)

- Proselytizing the Bible on TV while awaiting trial. (My man, Richard Scrushy of HealthSouth, read the Bible on a morning TV show called *Viewpoint* in Birmingham during his trial . . . in Birmingham. He began preaching in churches and invited pastors and followers to his trial. *Hallelujah, praise cheat-us!*)

- Ending affirmative action after getting a position to do so because of affirmative action. (Supreme Court

Justice Clarence "My book sold millions and I've got a job for life" Thomas.)
- Praising the free market while circumventing its rules. (Everybody ever born.)

**Succes$tory:** *"We fired Kate Moss for her cocaine bust. We took a moral stand! Us! The peddler of a chemical scent whose sole purpose is to deceive people into sexual relations. Ha!"* —Chanel

Looking for easy hypocrisy? Give to charity. Great Cheaters are some of the biggest contributors to local and national causes, and they often start their own, like Oprah's Angel Network, Bono's One Campaign, and Ken Lay's "Seriously, I'm not dead—I'm just hiding, but I'm running out of food" Foundation. These groups don't exist *just* to get tax breaks, nor are they *always* sham fronts to hide profits. Sometimes they simply work to get local communities to blindly love and forgive you, whether you're a corporate crook, an athlete with too much money, a movie star with guilt, or a retired lobbyist. A well-funded anti–cleft palates organization can help others turn the other cheek.

*"He seemed like such a nice guy. Always helping out around the neighborhood. Quiet, kept to himself. I never thought they'd find so many bodies in his basement."* —*Neighbors reacting to news of a serial killer and/or cheater living next door*

## Spin, Baby, Spin

You can fool all of the people some of the time and some of the people all of the time, and that's all you need to Get Rich Cheating.

Even though everything you've done up to this point is, in totality, positive—at least for *you*—some might not get the big picture. So, like the Great Cheaters, twist and turn your bad deeds into good things. It's possible to see events in many different ways: Ford either "lost an astounding $4 billion" or "kept their losses under $10 billion." Enron either "stole" or "arbitraged."

It's all a matter of perspective. Look at something, decide what you want it to mean, then unleash a tangled web of words and imagery to lead your audience to that conclusion. The Great Cheater knows that there's no such thing as bad publicity, only bad publicists. Omit certain facts, emphasize others, and always remain vague, obscure, and confusing. Good spinmeisters—be they spokesmen, publicists, or members of the corporate PR department—can take your foot out of your mouth and place it on the road to riches.

Spinning is the art of making something bad into something good and lucrative. To enhance their humanity and earning power, cheating celebrities (or their publicists) spin a drunken binge into dehydration, reckless driving and child endangerment into sleepless empathy with the victims of (insert most recent natural disaster), underage sex and child porn into "research for a book," anti-Semitism into alcoholism, racism into alcoholism, and, oddly, alcoholism into prescription painkiller addiction.

"Cozy" apartments, a "people person," "youthful indiscretions," "girls being girls." These are just some impressive everyday spin jobs. Other Great Cheater spin:

- For centuries, the White House spokesperson has helped ordinary people accept everything from the public health benefits of global warming (Dana Perino) to the really long nap Lincoln took after a show at the Ford Theater (Lincoln's press secretary).
- Ari Fleischer, Scott McClellan, Perino, Mike McCurry, and that guy from the movie *Thank You for Smoking* are among the great propagandists of our time, able to make trillions flow with the tip of their tongues. McClellan admitted his job was to deceive, twist, distort, and enable.* He did a good job.
- After Hurricane Katrina, President Bush touted economic recovery while speaking to disaster relief workers in North Carolina. Yes, business was booming for the catastrophe industry, but that's like saying the Detroit Lions are a success to people who sell the letter "L."
- You're not "avoiding taxes"; you're "increasing tax competitiveness."

---

* McClellan was later on the receiving end of the White House spin machine. He did dish it; he should be able to take it.

- You're not "cutting jobs"; you're just "lowering the retirement age (to now)."
- You can't make an omelet without breaking a few eggs.
- You're just expanding the limits of America's knowledge.
- Don't stifle innovation!
- "Hey! No one at GM has committed mass murder this week!"
- Stupidsayswhat?

Is your nose growing? Can you sell me the Brooklyn Bridge? Are your pants on fire? If so, you've got the spinning chops of a Great Cheater.

## Counterattack

If you've got a bad image—and by now you should deserve one—counter it with aggressive public relations (beyond just taking a picture of some cancer kids playing with kittens).

Timing counts. Pepsi hired an Indian CEO when it was facing public relations nightmares in her home country. Walmart, in the midst of the nation's largest sex discrimination suit, set up a $25 million fund to support women-owned businesses.

Walmart is a great example. They've got a political consulting group to counter their bad image. Civil Rights leader Andrew Young was the public face for a while, which prompted MLK Jr. and Rosa Parks to turn underground 360s. Rumor has it that the company's first move will be to jump around on Oprah's couch, telling everyone how much it loves fair labor standards. Next, an attack ad by Swift Mobile Home Veterans for Truth: "Anti-Walmart activists helped fund bin Laden." Then they'll announce that rival Kmart has yellowcake uranium and attack JCPenney.

That's not entirely true, but you believed it for a minute, right? That's the beauty of good PR. If Walmart can have a PR campaign, you'd better have one too.

## Distract and Destroy

Are people catching on to your schemes, seeking information, asking questions about your activities, wondering where you got those dead bodies? Well, as the good PR man knows, if something goes wrong, change the subject. Politicians do it all the time. Think anyone really cares about gay marriage, abortion, flag-burning, or the spotted owl? No, but these is-sues shift focus away from rampant corruption and ineffective leadership. In business, look to Sony BMG who, when rocked by a payola scandal, simply arrested a bunch of thirteen-year-olds for downloading music.

This is the public we're talking about. They've got the at-tention span of a gnat on Red Bull. You get in trouble, show 'em something that sparkles. Here are some surefire distrac-tions to save your behind:

## Get Rich Cheating

- Adopt a peculiar physical attribute and news reports will waste words and space on it. The guy with the hook hand, limp, and horns did, um . . . he's got a hook hand, limp, and horns!
- If you're a woman, even better. Every report will focus on your clothes first, accessories second, hair and makeup third, and evil misdeeds in a footnote.*
- "Sure, there's $3 billion unaccounted for, but *24* jumped the shark, and can you believe (young person) got knocked off *American Idol*?"

---

\* If there's room for it, White Oprah.

# 23

# Marketing Madness

### Limited Time Offer,
### While Supplies Last
### (Which They Won't)

**P**ublic relations is not only about image. Great Cheaters pursue every available angle to get people to love them, to *need* them. They know how to ride public relations to the bank by manipulating customers' values, beliefs, and behavior and convincing them to buy, buy, buy, buy. Bait and switch, pull their heartstrings with babies and puppies and babies holding puppies, make them feel guilty, prey on their human frailty, insecurities, yearning, and desires, shill, use viral marketing, celebrity endorsements, spam, pyramid schemes, and subliminal (touch it) sexual imagery.

## Invest in the Future
Prepare for tomorrow's customers, employees, and slaves by ingratiating yourself with them today. The Great Cheater

lurks around every schoolyard, eyeing each child, waiting for a wandering wee one to fall into his trap.

- Target children directly—"Cartoon sponges might be gay, but cartoon camels don't sell cigarettes!"—or with something shiny: The FDA approved the use of colorful pills for certain prescription drugs. Wouldn't it be a shame if kids thought they were candy? A real $hame.

- Hasbro has a new version of Monopoly with "classic" items like a Toyota Prius, New Balance sneakers, McDonald's fries, and a Motorola cell phone. *Never too early to brand fun.*

- The Walt Disney Company makes a cell phone that tracks kids via GPS. Disney tracking children. That way they can be sure kids see enough Disney movies advertising Disney products that are derivatives of Disney movies advertising Disney products.

- Who's the spokesman for MetLife? Snoopy. *Yup.* Life insurance, death, and cartoon dogs: the Holy Trinity. Way to get kids thinking about mortality and your products, MetLife.

- BMW gave a $10 million endowment gift to the Clemson Graduate Engineering Center. Stanford, Princeton, and Berkeley are among schools similarly partnered with corporations like ExxonMobil, GE, Toyota, BP, and Novartis. Heck, my law school classrooms were named after corporate law firms. They say every man has his price. Schools do too. Great way to have grateful, eager, buried-in-debt twenty-year-olds prepared to do your bidding.

## Certify It!

Create a phony organization to certify your product with an official-looking logo. The Great Cheaters do it. "100% Organic," "A Healthy Smart Choice Selection," "Environmentally Friendly," or "Certified by the Council for Good Things That Make You Happy." Upon closer examination, the only thing these organizations review are *your* products. So what? How many times have I told you: People are dumb.

Environmental products are superhot right now, so just label your stuff "green." Doesn't matter if it's true or not—just claim you recycle. Heck, charge extra to do so. Some call this "greenwashing" because you'll have so much money you'll leave some in your pants when you send 'em to the cleaners.

## Cult

Create a cultlike following for your company. Use catchphrases and code words to make yourself indispensable to your customers' sense of self-worth. Look at Barack Obama with "hope" and "change"; Apple with the iPod, iTunes, the Nano; Starbucks with Grande, Venti, Vidi, Vici. No one understands it, but the message is, "If you don't get it, you're not cool. You'll be left out in the cold while we party with lingerie models who love indie rock and know the secret to everlasting life."

## Patriotism

It's the last refuge of the damned and the first stop for a good advertising firm.

- Ever wonder what Chevy has to do with America and the civil rights movement? Chevy doesn't wonder. They're too busy counting their loot from those John Mellencamp "This Is Our Country" commercials.
- The Army's "Army of One" campaign, marketing of video games, and offers of cosmetic surgery* make it seem like military service is just a big respect party for go-getters (*After-party in Tehran!*). Not too much mention of the death and destruction.
- Even old friend Walmart has an advertising campaign that includes the line, "Twenty-three hundred dollars a year, which buys a lot of things—and a whole lot of freedom." There you have it. Money = freedom = buying things. *I'm glad someone finally had the nerve to say it.*

## Fear Profiteering

Raw emotions are the best source for irrational consumer behavior. Scare people into buying your product. *You will DIE if you do not BUY my product!* Bird flu has killed just a few people around the world, but *Quick! Buy Donald Rumsfeld's*

---

* Karen Schaler, "All That You Can Be," *The New Yorker*, July 26, 2004.

*Tamiflu.*\* Remember the London airport "threat," which prevented us from taking liquids on planes? *Just a plot by the toothpaste and shampoo industry.* You know the color-coded terror alert system in place since 9/11? *A marketing ploy of rainbow suspenders producers.*

Be prepared for the future of fear. In ten years or so, clean water will be scarce. Invest in a water bottling company. Then prepare a news segment: *Tonight at 11: Water. Is your family safe, or are they just drinking H$_2$-uh-oh?*

## Addictions Can Be Habit (Spending) Forming

Some Great Cheaters adopt a drug dealer mentality—"First one's free!"—to get people physically and psychologically addicted to their product, and then they jack up the prices. Soda machines in schools, Starbucks' caffeine content, and the entire tobacco industry are the obvious examples. But consider these In$pirations:

- Nestlé bought Jenny Craig. A sweets-maker buying a diet empire. It's like heroin producers chipping in for a methadone clinic. "The sooner they get thin, the sooner they can get fat again." Smart move on the part of Nestlé, hedging its bets like that, since people will probably just fluctuate between fat and thin. (I wonder if original Black White Oprah's an investor.)

---

\* The former Defense secretary owns at least $5 million of stock in Gilead, the company that developed Tamiflu.

- Sure, Google and Microsoft own most of creation (*See* Oxygen.Google.com, or Microsoft's Carbon-Based Life-Form 2.1), but what about unheralded firms like the Carlyle Group, a politically connected company that specializes in defense, energy, and telecommunications? They've also purchased portions of Nielsen and Dunkin' Donuts and who knows what else. Donuts, market research, strategic oil and military operations . . . *Oh my, the next source of energy is body fat! It's people! My plasma TV is people!*
- Certain vendors make themselves indispensable, selling copiers or voting machines or computers that constantly break, then providing exclusive, expensive services to fix, install, train, supply, maintain, wash, lather, rinse, cash in, escape, repeat.
- Make sure your main product requires purchase of all of your secondary, but more expensive, products. Microsoft notoriously bundled everything so you needed the latest Microsoft software to prevent Microsoft viruses on your Microsoft hardware and your Microsoft PDA and your Microsoft life!

It's sort of like when your mother cleans your apartment. She'll intentionally put items in illogical places just so you have to call her for help. Great Cheaters do the same thing, except where your mom gets love and guilt, they get money. *Psst, if you get enough of one, you can buy the other.*

# Google Was Originally Called "Backrub." Really.

If you get an unshakable bad reputation or receive less-than-favorable publicity or just aren't selling enough, simply change your name and reintroduce your company as something different. Bausch & Lomb took its long-wear Optima lenses and just renamed them Medalist in order to enter the more lucrative disposable lens market. Philip Morris changed its name to Altria, Diebold is now Premier Election Solutions, Arthur Andersen's going by Accenture, for some reason Lindsay Lohan is still Lindsay Lohan, and the major manufacturers of asbestos briefly considered calling their product "lung candy."

Remember: A fraud by any other name would still cheat as sweet.

# Confusion to Your Enemies

Confusion is key to any successful marketing and PR campaign. Some will misconstrue incomprehensibility as intelligence. They'll assume you know what you're talking about and they'll give you money. Plus, confusion prevents people from knowing what you're up to: The less sense you make, the better your chance of getting away with it.

## The Tyranny of Mumbo Jumbo

Build an impenetrable wall of obscure language. Lawyers, doctors, insurance companies, and auto mechanics do it. What the hell are they talking about? You don't know, *I* don't know, and chances are *they* don't know. But we pay them extra because they sound smart. "Placentas" and "carburetors?" *Yeah, like those really exist.* Why do you think Latin is still around? So lawyers can make money objecting like Whack-a-Moles. A "writ of habeas corpus?" *Whatever, Perry Mason, here's a dollar.* Trust me. I'm a lawyer.

## Politics Is Hard

Politicians want to maintain power to keep stealing and cheating and frequenting D.C. madams. So they all perpetrate the myth that politics is hard to understand, that there's no difference between Republicans and Democrats, that we really shouldn't take off work on a Tuesday just to vote. They keep us disinterested and confused so we don't look behind the curtain and see the bald man operating the giant head that sticks it to the girl with the pigtails and the dog in the basket. *You know, the Dick Cheney of Oz.*

## Financial Blabbering

Financial reports are loaded with columns, numbers, and words. Make it madness with a maze of nonsense. Just grab a pen, a comfy chair, and start making things up. Make a game of it, challenging yourself to come up with new words. Where do you think "synergy" came from? It's all rhythm. *Words words words, punctuation, numbers numbers numbers, footnotes,\* words words words, repeat.* It may seem crazy, but,

---

\* I steal money from little old ladies.

remember, if they think you're crazy, they won't think you're cheating.

Lies are an increasingly large portion of financial statements. Look at the percentages in this chart.

## Composition of Corporate Financial Statements, 2009

What's in the Pie?

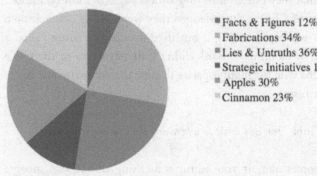

- Facts & Figures 12%
- Fabrications 34%
- Lies & Untruths 36%
- Strategic Initiatives 15%
- Apples 30%
- Cinnamon 23%

Every good financial report has lots of charts, just like every good fourth-grade book report had a clear plastic binder. Presentation says a lot, and charts can say whatever you want them to.

It's all about perspective, my cheating friend. Don't allow them to have any.

## The Truth? Maybe They *Can* Handle the Truth

You could always drown your adversaries in a sea of confusion by disclosing everything in an unwieldy and incomprehensible way. Every penny, every detail. Simply overwhelm them so they won't be able to see the conniving, treacherous, deceitful forest for the trees . . . trees cut down to make paper printed with nonsense.

Enron execs basically disclosed what they were doing; it's just that they buried it in fifty zillion pages of mumbo jumbo. Plenty of CEOs acknowledged they were selling off their own stock while promoting it but used an obscure filing called a Form 5. Commerce Bank didn't hide payments to the CEO and his wife for inappropriate things; the company just made it confusing.

**Huh?** *"You did what to whose dog for how many cookies?"*\*

Sometimes, if you admit something outrageous, people will be so caught off guard they'll either think you're kidding, ignore it, or actually consider you a good guy for being forthright. If you decide to reveal the truth, just put it someplace hard to find: Asterisks, footnotes, and charts . . . *oh my!*

---

\*   Sir Alex of Afterman, letter to author, 1999.

# 24

## Great Expectations

### Oliver Twist's Got Nothing on You

A big part of obscuring your cheating is being able to shape what people expect of your work. We all have expectations. You expect to get rich, but you can't do so without manipulating the expectations of others.

*Why?* Well, one of the great things about economics is that it's complete nonsense. Allow me to steal another old joke:

> *A physicist, a geologist, and an economist are stranded on an island with one can of food and no can opener. The physicist suggests heating the can until it pops open, the geologist wants to smash the can with a rock, and the economist says, "Let's assume we have a can opener."*

These "economists" are the people whose opinions help the brave entrepreneur Get Rich Cheating every earnings period. A company can make a billion dollars, but the stock price will fall if the gain is short of analysts' "expectations." Read any report about a company's performance, and it will mention expectations followed by market reaction. It doesn't matter what the company does—profit, loss, genocidal rampage—if it beats expectations, the stock price goes up and you get rich.

I used to fight this "Cult of Expectations." Why are expectations so important? Why do we give so much power to modern-day soothsayers? Isn't "better than expected" a fairly arbitrary and self-serving standard? *Honey, I know I got home drunk at four a.m. last night, but I neither crashed the car, nor did I cheat on you . . . and I thought I would, so it's really better than expected.* How could anyone take a prediction so seriously? When I was seven, I predicted I'd be a fireman, by fifteen a ballplayer, but at twenty-two my three-a.m.-Cartoon-Network-watching career put the kibosh on those forecasts.

My own attitude toward expectations changed one dramatic financial quarter. A company I'd invested in posted massive losses (they had no product) but the stock price rose . . . because it was better than expected. What were people expecting? It was insane, but it had made me rich. Just like the Great Cheaters, I learned to embrace the Cult of Expectations. So should you.

When you're done embracing it, put it to work. Manage expectations to maximize your cheating gains. If you outperform expectations, you'll be considered a success, so simply keep expectations low. Start a whisper campaign about you and your company's mental, physical, and financial health; walk around in sweatpants (take it from me, no one expects much from someone in sweats); talk about your antipsychotic medication and how you've always let down your parents, lovers, and friends. Then, when you announce that you didn't destroy the plant or burn the product or forfeit the season, you'll beat expectations, your value will jump, and you'll cash out. Just be sure to backdate your stock options (See Chapter 13: Numbers Never Lie) to the low point, around the day you said, "I hope we recover from the locusts."

It's all about expectations in every industry. Hollywood bigwigs do it, lowering the projected income so that *Ishtar*, *Waterworld*, and *Gigli* can be called successes . . . and then that studio can get more money to produce more crap. *People are dumb!* Athletes predict doom and failure so that their inevitable victories are more dramatic, their story more compelling, their shoe deals worth more to impoverished third-world children.

Politicians routinely lower predictions and downplay poor performance. Barack Obama lost the West Virginia primary by forty or so points, but "expected" to lose by sixty plus, so it was a success. Before every political debate, candidates talk up the other side's skills and talk down their own. Cheater of the free world George W. Bush's 2000 campaign portrayed him as a simpleton with few political skills, and Sarah Palin's predebate threshold in 2008 was the ability to stay upright, so pundits literally said they both did "better than expected."

What were they expecting? A three-headed lava monster that eats nuns and soccer moms? *They're morons, but at least our women haven't been devoured by a fiery mutant.*

A Great Cheater also uses expectations to attract investors, customers, and their money. When pitching your company to them, be optimistic and, most important, theoretical. You "could" earn billions. Possibly. Potentially. Probably. When Enron accounted for more than ten years of imaginary future profits, that was theory in action.

Send out spam, promote yourself in chat rooms and on MySpace. Conrad Black posted on a Yahoo! message board to pump up the stock of his Hollinger International. Same basic thing goes for the CEO of Whole Foods Inc., who talked up his company and denigrated its chief competitor under a pseudonym. When the stock of that company, Wild Oats, was low enough, he tried to buy. While you're "not supposed to" do that, he did. Anonymously. So, have at it.

You must simply manipulate what everyone believes about you. How you might perform, what you might do, what ditch you might end up in after a bender. Their expectations determine just how rich you can cheat.

## Talking Heads

How do you manage expectations through the flow and nature of information about you? Don't change the message—control the messenger. Toll Brothers actually bought newspapers, including the *Philadelphia Inquirer* and *Daily*

*News*, which will all soon publish the ongoing series "Giving Money to Toll Brothers Keeps Your Family Safe." You don't have to actually own a media outlet like they do, but if you want to Get Rich Cheating, it's vital that you harness the power of the media.

The greatest bull market in history ran from the summer of 1982 to the end of the twentieth century—and then again in the 2000s—thanks to a wave of unfounded optimism. It wasn't called a "bull market" for nothing: The growth was largely based upon, oh, what's that word . . . the uh . . . fabrications . . . um . . . untruths . . . uh . . . fudged info . . . *the Bull!* It was the b.s. statements of analysts and reporters that hypnotized desperate investors into believing in infinite riches.

Remember Netscape? Before its IPO, its shares were valued at about $14 each. With the hype and buzz machine in full swing, the offering *opened* at $71. Where is it now? Nobody knows. Where are the founders who fed the hype machine? Probably paying someone to stop their male pattern baldness.

Words alone can still make you millions. One well-placed tidbit of breaking news reported on some obscure website can change fortunes in an instant. That's why you've got to cultivate relationships with the hundreds of talking heads who litter the landscape. Remember Maria Bartiromo, the CNBC "Money Honey" of the mid-nineties? Of course not, you only got into business the day you picked up this book. Just trust me (I'm a you-know-what)—she was powerful.

People listened to her then and they listen to her now. So get someone like her. Whether or not you stoop to the level of hiring eye candy that you know hard-up, socially awkward, and misogynistic brokers will watch just for the titillation is at your discretion.

Reporters in every field are just like you. They want to make it big and they want to make it quick. You promise them the inside scoops that will propel them to stardom, and they'll be favorable. You throw in some stock, and they'll be lovable. You prepackage and produce news segments about your company so they don't have to work, and they'll marry you. If you kick execs off your private jet to fly reporters across the ocean like Citibank's Todd Thomson did, why, my media-savvy friend, they'll be Maria Bartiromo.

Those covering politics are easily swayed to your position. Political advisors become political pundits advocating political positions of political advisors: Another revolutionary revolving door of wealth and influence. George Stephanopoulos is a former Clinton right-hand man and hair model; Karl Rove was Bush's brain; retired generals tout the wisdom of military plans; James Carville, Donna Brazile, and Paul Begala are all advisors to or supporters of various politicians. They all appear on TV as analysts and experts, rarely mentioning their connections, while getting themselves and their friends understood, elected, and rich. Is it fair? You say "potato," I say "cheating."

Sports and entertainment reporters are generally failed

athletes and entertainers themselves. They say those who can't do, teach. Well, those who can't do and are bitter about it report. Sweeten their bitterness with a smile, wink, bribe, joke, or promise to introduce them to your agent. They'll love you, and you'll reap the benefits.

Oh sure, journalism critics claim this is some sort of a conflict of interest, but "conflict of interest" is just another phrase for "inventive resource allocation." Come on, who are viewers going to trust? Someone with no stake in the news, or someone who's got a lot riding on what they say?

Sometimes the talking heads who help corporate crooks Get Rich Cheating aren't reporters but analysts with financial stakes in the stocks they discuss. Superstars of the 1990s like Merrill Lynch's Henry Blodget and Salomon Smith Barney's Jack Grubman, Mary Meeker, and Abby Joseph Cohen pumped up stocks they or their firms owned. Frequently, what they said publicly didn't match how they acted privately. At one point, two-thirds of all analysts' recommendations were buys, and only 1 percent were sells.* Guess what? They had their fingers crossed. If viewers couldn't see the fingers, that's their problem. Caveat investor.**

Even *Mad Money* guru Jim Cramer admitted that he'd manipulated stock prices in the past via rumors and reporters.

---

* Yes, aspiring cheat, there are now rules about investment banks both owning and analyzing stocks. Firms have to construct what's called a "Chinese wall" between ownership and analysts, blah, blah, blah. Between you and me, the Chinese wall is much like those Chinese thumbcuffs—easy to get around once you know the trick. (The trick: Pretend the wall doesn't exist.)

** "Look out, chumps."

In this case, "mad" means "awesome." Mad, dope, rockin', far out, groovy, tubular . . . all the hip phrases kids use today, and with which you should get rich tomorrow.

## Prove It

In order to spread your message of cheat, your talking heads will need "evidence," "proof," "authority," or "a house of cards." These are the "talking points" repeated ad nauseam by identically airbrushed blowhards. Oftentimes, these points are provided by "independent studies" that the Great Cheater himself has guided. For instance, a 2006 study finding that lung cancer could be prevented by using CAT scans—*Smoke away, consumers!*—was underwritten by a $3.6 million grant from Liggett Group, which makes Liggett Select, Eve, Grand Prix, Quest, and Pyramid cigarettes. Municipal unions in New York routinely hired Jonathan Schwartz to run accounting analysis for legislative bills, and his analyses were always pro-union and misstated costs by only $500 million. Merck wrote the studies in which doctors endorsed their drugs. Merck printed the reports, docs signed 'em; then Merck wrote checks, docs deposited 'em, little Timmy took Vioxx and died. It's not so much the circle of life, but sorta the triangle of cheat.

Lies are good authority too. In 1998, several witnesses told Congress about suffering at the hands of an abusive Internal Revenue Service. It was all made up. The testimony was provided as evidence for changes that would benefit their patrons.

They did what they needed to do to pass what they needed to pass. Just because the stories weren't true doesn't mean a lot of people didn't get or stay rich because of their telling. And isn't the art of storytelling all about getting rich?

"Think tanks" are the *best* source of cheating authority. Like toilet tanks, think tanks will take your crap and clean it up. You want to pass a bill that shows killing hoboes improves the working conditions of Indonesian amputees? Give the Council on Environmental Quality two weeks and it'll be on your desk in triplicate. They accept American Express. What are some Great Cheaters' favorite think tanks?

- The promanagement Heritage Foundation puts out subtle studies like "How to Close Down the Department of Labor."
- The American Enterprise Institute is "the premier scholarly institution of the conservative movement." It publishes Newt Gingrich and Robert Bork and the board includes such pursuers of intellectual honesty and economic fairness as the CEOs of ExxonMobil, Dow Chemical, State Farm Insurance, and American Express. Simply fund scholarly research that opposes regulation, corporate taxation, and taxes on the wealthy. Enterprising indeed.
- American Center for Voting Rights was a front to make us think there's lots of voter fraud, even though there isn't. BUT! Their studies do enable the passage of legisla-

tion that allows for disenfranchisement of voters who would be against the interests of the Center's funders, so, in a way, it's a self-fulfilling prophecy of cheat.

- Somebody spent a lot of time convincing the country that the media is liberal, so there's been a generation of conservative rule, which, really, explains this whole book.

The names of your institutes don't matter, and should, in fact, be as deceptive as possible. The Employment Policies Institute is funded by the restaurant industry and has shown that raising minimum wage will lead to another Great Depression; the Healthy Forests Initiative advocated the cutting of trees; the Clear Skies Initiative promotes pollution; and it's very likely that the Unity People's Front Fighting for Puppies wants to ensure the mutilation of puppies for sport.

Think tanks are big business. The budgets of the American Enterprise Institute, Brookings Institution, Cato Institute, Center for American Progress, Center for Strategic and International Studies, Council on Foreign Relations, and Heritage Foundation are all in the $20 to $60 million neighborhood.[*] That's a nice neighborhood, right next to the one with those ballplayers with gigantic heads. So, if you're not enlisting a think tank to be your irrefutable evidence, then be a think tank yourself.

[*] Elisabeth Bumiller, "Research Groups Boom in Washington," *The New York Times*, January 30, 2008.

Either way, think tanks will help you Get Rich Cheating. *Don't forget to flush.*

# Don't Agree to Disagree

If you can't get reporters to parrot pro-you opinions, at least eliminate the anti-you voice. Vladimir Putin (Russian president, prime minister, and Tough Guy for Life) had opponents digitally removed from television shows.* Just erased 'em, like they never existed and never challenged his cheating ways. He also consolidated the media into a unified propaganda voice behind the Kremlin in ways that would be the envy of media *conglomerators* like Ted Turner (CNN, TBS, TNT, Jane Fonda closed-circuit spy cam), Michael Bloomberg (Bloomberg News, Bloomberg Terminals, Bloomberg Messaging, Bloomberg TV, Bloomberg New York City), and anyone else who might own newspapers, radio stations, TV networks, and, say, publishing companies all around the world.

So get yourself some people who love the sound of their own voice—analysts and reporters—and put 'em in your pocket. Have them praise you on the talk shows, radio, newspapers, chat rooms, and blogs. The Great Cheaters know you should never stop telling people how wonderful you are, because, if you say it often enough, eventually it becomes true . . . and makes you all rich.

---

* Clifford J. Levy, "It Isn't Magic: Putin Opponents Are Made to Vanish from TV," *The New York Times,* June 3, 2008.

# 25

## Hall of Fame

### Great Cheaters on Mount Richmore

We all have heroes. John F. Kennedy, Willie Mays, Jenna Jameson. Mine can be found here, in the Cheaters' Hall of Fame.

These are the industries that I consider the gold standard. The Greatest of the Great Cheaters. They've so institutionalized the Get Rich Cheating methods, you could have just skipped the first part of this book and joined one of them . . . which is why I buried this chapter back here. Poppa's gotta eat.*

## Pharmaceuticals

Taking the drug dealer mentality to the limit, they sell drugs and want nothing more than to keep doing so. Pfizer recently had to unload its consumer health division, since "consumer

---

\* These are just *industries* that are perfect cheaters. Some Great Cheaters—Enron, the 1919 Chicago White Sox, Pam Anderson, the AMPTP, Richard Nixon, Bill Clinton, George W. Bush, Rod Blagojevich, the NFL owners—might've made a specific Hall of Fame, but not this time.

health" runs counter to the industry's core value of manufacturing disease and facilitating addiction.

### Succes$tory: *"We make it Bad so we can make it Better."* —Drug companies

They make sure everyone's hooked on something. Walmart offers thirty-day trials of certain drugs for $4.* Drug companies employ an army of ex-cheerleaders to go around to strung-out doctors offering free gifts and lunches and conferences full of more cheerleaders and booze and praise and love and booze and praise and love. In return, they just ask the doctors to prescribe unnecessary and addictive treatments. *You're itchy? Get on this regimen of eighty pills a day.* No able-to-pay patient should have to face life with only food, shelter, entertainment, and love.

Of course, drug companies are also the kings of self-perpetuating cycles of addiction:

John Q. Public: "I'm so stressed out, I can't sleep."

    Big Pharma: "Have some Ambien."

John Q. Public: "Thanks. Um, Ambien makes me eat in my sleep, and I'm gaining all this weight."

---

\*   "First one's free."

# Get Rich Cheating

```
Big Pharma:    "Have a diet pill, like
                TrimSpa."


John Q. Public: "Thanks, but TrimSpa's full
                of adrenaline and caffeine, so
                now I can't sleep . . ."


Big Pharma:    "Have some Ambien."
```

Repeat until John Q. maxes out his credit cards.

Genentech, Pfizer, Eli Lilly. These are your heroes. They don't just sit around and wait for us to fall into their trap. No, these geniuses actively stalk their prey, spending between $11 and $30 billion on advertising (depending on who's counting).

*The poor?* Sure. Heroic drug companies have been reaping a Medicare plan windfall by selling drugs to the poor. *Drugs for poor people? Watch out, CIA, you've got competition!*

*The young?* Colorful prescription drugs, Flintstones vitamins, Ritalin that is so, so sweet . . . *It's a learning tool! It's an addiction! It's a seizure!*

*The dying?* You bet. Genentech's got a cancer treatment that costs $100,000 a year. They defend the price, citing the inherent value of "life-sustaining therapies." For instance, Genentech's execs need massage therapy, group therapy, caviar therapy . . .

You have to admire an industry with the vision to profit

from the last hopes of the damned. Come on, what else are these companies gonna do? Move to Boca and sell penny stocks? No, they're gonna Get Rich Cheating. They already have.

Big pharma's got the government regulation game down too, paying off generic competitors and routinely tweaking their formulations just enough to maintain the patent that protects their exclusive cash inflow. Isn't that right, Claritin and Prilosec, er, ah, I mean, Clarinex and Nexium? (I forget which are the new names you made up.)

Drugs are a multibillion-dollar industry, but they don't cure cancer and AIDS. No, no, no, they make Viagra and Zoloft. So we can be hard, but numb. "Oh honey, this sex is so . . . *meh*." Why? Because you'll make a lot more money playing to the male sexual ego, depression, insecurity, and superficiality than just fixing boring real problems.

They're so good, they can sell us stuff we don't even need. "Restless leg syndrome"? Never heard of it until GlaxoSmith-Kline told me it was a serious problem; now I have to buy a two-year supply of their Requip medication. It's easier than amputation. Pfizer basically created the disease fibromyalgia in order to sell Lyrica, the first drug approved to treat it. Do you have it? No? *You will.*

I swear, if I could, I would make millions with one product and a simple advertising campaign: "Not blissfully happy at all times? Ask your doctor about the new once-a-day Stop Hitting Yourself.® Stop Hitting Yourself.® Why are you hitting yourself?"

I guess what I'm trying to say is, like all Great Cheaters, I love drugs and, uh, drug companies.

# Oil

ExxonMobil's 2007 annual profit was the largest in U.S. history . . . At least since ExxonMobil's 2006 profit, which was the largest since 2005, which is pretty sweet, right? The company earned about $4.5 million per hour, $1,300 per second. I challenge you to cheat any richer than that.

> **Succes$tory:** *"It's no big deal, I mean, we've still got to pay taxes. Ha ha ha ha ha! No, but seriously, it's hard being Big Oil. Venezuela is offering to give it away, people pretend to conserve, and we've got all these piles of money to spend. I mean, it's not like we can invest it in America . . . Look, Dubai has an indoor ski slope. We've got a lot of catching up to do."*
>
> —Big Oil

Oil is a classic cartel, led by the Organization of the Petroleum Exporting Countries, or D.O.O.M. If you join them, not only do you get to control supply—and therefore price and profit—but you can wreak havoc on the markets just by pumping out a few rumors.

```
"Hey, I found a bunch of oil!"
    Stock price . . . UP!
```

"Uh-oh, trouble in Iran." *Cost of oil . . . UP!*

"I don't feel so good, kind of unstable."
  *Cost of oil . . . UP!*

"You better watch out, you better not cry, you
  better not shout, I'm telling you why."
  *Cost of Christmas . . . UP!*

Great Cheaters relish the randomness of oil prices. It's an elastic-pricing theory, based on beating customers into submission, a.k.a. "adjusting market expectations":

$5? *No way!*
$3? *Okay . . .*
$10? *No way!*
$7? *Okay . . .*
My whole family? *No way!*
Just my daughter? *Okay . . .*

Hey, prices have to be high, right? Lee Raymond's $144,000-per-day deal from ExxonMobil isn't going to pay for itself. Come on, America. Come together and sacrifice. Think of the children. The little oily children.

If you do manage to get your hands on an oil company, you too will be the darling of the government, always finding some way to block taxes and fines. A General Accounting Office report predicted over *$80 billion* in government receipts could be lost to energy industry incentives over the next twenty-five years. *EIGHTY BILLION DOLLARS*! Enough to be in all caps *and* italicized! Just for having some buddies in office.

Sure, every now and then the government gives in to defeatist wacko liberal tree-huggers and slaps an energy company on the wrist. In the summer of 2006, a Senate panel approved a $5 billion profit tax on the oil industry, though, per tradition, the senators did so while winking. The old Wink Tax. *Oh no, $5 billion out of $200 billion in profits! Call Sally Struthers for a phone-a-thon.*

Oil is a safe investment for an aspiring cheat. Americans will never wean ourselves off with alternatives like ethanol. Even if we did, we'd then be beholden to the corn lobby, and before you know it, we'd be invading Iowa to prevent them from plowing under their cornfields. *If you build it, he will come . . . and raise gas prices.*

## Credit Cards

Another sweet racket of the Great Cheaters, based upon people's greed and desperation. Give everyone access to credit without regard to their credit worthiness. Send them fifteen invitations a day. Arbitrarily hike up interest rates and transaction fees ("You looked at me funny: 29 percent APR"). Get your chums in Congress to end personal bankruptcy. Then watch the money, favors, and first-born sons come marching in.

*Competition*? Yeah, you tell me the difference between Visa, MasterCard, Discover, or the rest.

*Identity theft*? Make people afraid of that. Report arbitrary, accidental losses of data on millions of customers. Charge ten bucks a month for "protection." If they don't buy it, send over Tony and Vito to rough 'em up a bit.

*Make smart hires.* Louis Freeh, former head of the FBI, worked for MBNA credit card services, where they actually have more reliable information than at his former gig. Why would a credit card company need a spy? To get rich.

*Hard to get in the game*? Nope. The House recently allowed any credit-rating company in business for three years to become a "nationally recognized statistical rating organization." *Phew.* Come 2010, we'll be protected by Pedro's Credit Rating Service and Auto Supply.

## Television
The real opiate of the masses. Many of its records have since been broken, but television, or "TV" to its friends, changed the way the game was played. TV brought cheating right into the homes of every customer, investor, and employee. TV dumbed them down, eliminated their imagination, trivialized hard work, made instant riches and fame just a "makeover" or contest away, sanitized and centralized information, raised standards of beauty and superficiality to unattainable heights, and gave everyone a false sense of commonality . . . all so that the Great Cheaters could take advantage of them.

Thank you, TV. *Thank you.*

# 26

## The Financial Crisis

### A Get Rich Cheating Case Study

The financial "crisis" that exploded in the fall of 2008 provides a wonderful example of how many of the tenets of Get Rich Cheating work together to make some people very rich and others incredibly poor. Ideas in action. Seriously, this thing had it all. Virtually every page of this book was represented in this, perhaps, the Greatest of All Cheats. It was the culmination of years of hard work by dedicated Great Cheaters and I thank them for making this book eternally relevant.

## The Basics

The whole situation is a little complicated, so allow me to uncomplicate some of it.

Local banks gave mortgages to people who couldn't afford them. The banks then sold those mortgages to other banks, which bundled them together into complex financial vehicles, which were then combined with other financial junk and sold to, and traded among, banks, municipalities, funds, and investors. All this activity made the stock market grow, which made the value of everyone's stuff—stocks, real estate, dreams—grow too. Since everyone's stuff was worth so much, everyone kept getting more credit, taking out more loans, buying more stuff . . . which got the market to keep growing and growing and growing. Each bad mortgage was another piece of bubble gum jammed into the swollen mouth of an economy that blows . . .

But then (*dramatic music, please!*), people stopped paying the mortgages they couldn't afford back in step one. So, like a house of cards built on stilts along the Gulf Coast during hurricane season, the whole thing collapsed. The mortgages weren't worth anything, so neither were the bundled mortgages, the combined financial gimmicks, the investments, the market increase, the stuff everyone owned, or the easy credit. *Kaput.* No more value, no more lending, no more nothing. People lost their homes, their investments, their sanity. Big firms like Bear Stearns, Lehman Brothers, AIG, Merrill Lynch, Citibank, and Wachovia collapsed, were sold, or had to be rescued. Soon enough, world governments started pouring in billions of dollars to fix the problem, and here were we, licking our chops and waiting to get rich off the fix.

*But how did everyone Get Rich Cheating along the way?*

Oh, financial crisis, how do I love thee? Let me recount the ways . . .

## Exploiting Everyone*

The whole thing was based upon cheaters exploiting desperate average people. (And "people" are what? *Dumb.***) The "American Dream" is home ownership, but that is totally impractical for most—that's why it's a dream. A dream that provided plenty of low-hanging fruit for cheating gardeners to pick with subprime loans.

> **Le$$on:** *Subprime loans are those made at extremely low—or "subprime"—introductory interest rates. The rates later balloon, but the teasers fool people who don't understand what they're signing and inevitably can't pay the higher rates.*

Listen to the pleasant sound of money being made:

- Local bankers and real estate agents earned fees and commissions steering home buyers into these mortgages with abusive, costly, and deceptive terms. *Ching!*
- They got more money as fees and penalties whenever these homeowners tried to get out of or refinance the mortgages. *Cha-ching!*
- Then they sold these mortgages to financial institutions and investment banks and washed their hands of them. *Cha-cha-ching!*

---

\* See Chapter 11.
\*\* See every chapter.

# Spin*

These mortgage lenders weren't predatory or dishonest but rather noble, selfless businessmen who gave the joy of home ownership to those who couldn't otherwise achieve the American dream. They made dreams come true . . . just like witches who lure kids into a gingerbread house and then shove 'em in the oven. Sure, they made some "mistakes," but they got rich and so did their friends and colleagues, and that's all that matters. Also, FYI, oven-baked little children are *deeeeee-licious*.

# Accounting Schemes**

There were so many accounting gimmicks involved in the housing bubble, credit crisis, and bailout that it's hard to single out just one for special recognition. From Countrywide Financial home lenders to Bear Stearns, Great Cheaters hid risk, undervalued debt, and simply made up numbers. Bubble-era hedge fund KL Group raised $194 million from investors just by saying it earned 100 percent from 2002 to 2005, when really, *ooops*, it lost $63 million. *Hey, you gotta practice lying to make perfect lying.* New Century Financial made zillions in the home lending market by creatively accounting for all their bad mortgages. They called their scheme to book imaginary future profits "gain on sale," which was less cumbersome than the original title, "We gave billions to people with subprime credit and assumed they'd never default because, well, we're morons."

---

\*    See Chapter 22.
\*\*   See Chapter 14.

**In$piration:** *"The thing about gain on sale account-
ing is that you can create a machine that just manu-
factures earnings out of thin air."*

—Richard Benson, Specialty Finance Group[*]

Don't you want a machine like that?

The securities tied to these subprime mortgages caused
wildly unpredictable price swings because they were new,
never-before-traded products. Since they'd never been traded,
there was no market for them, no way to set a price. So the
Great Cheaters simply defined their own market, set their
own prices, and watched the money pour in from a world
eager to be fooled. Their accounting method: EBSMM (Everybody Better Send Me Money).

# Confusion and Nondisclosure[**]

Those subprime loans that started the whole mess were designed not to be understood and were intended to be unaffordable, so that they would be refinanced for additional fees.
The banks and agents knew what they were doing . . . and
knew that the borrowers didn't know what they knew, or that
they didn't know they knew they didn't know they knew they
didn't know. *You know?*

Higher up the subprime chain, the financial derivative
MBSs, CDOs, and SIVs that caused so much trouble were

---

[*]   Lynnley Browning, "Accounting Said to Hide Lender Losses," *The New York Times*,
May 1, 2007.

[**]   See Chapters 21 and 22.

basically packaged subprime loans that everyone traded, but no one understood.

- MBSs are mortgage-backed securities whose cash flows are backed by, well, payments of a set of mortgage loans.
- CDOs are collateralized debt obligations, an un-regulated asset-backed security and structured credit product, constructed from a portfolio of fixed-income assets.
- SIVs are structured investment vehicles, or funds that borrow money by issuing short-term securities at low interest and then buying long-term securities at higher interest.

*Whaaaaaaa? Huh? Hmm?*

Even sophisticated investors were fooled by fancy financial language into thinking they were getting better deals than they really were.

"Credit default swaps" were also pretty confusing, and, for an ambitious cheater, pretty awesome. They basically were trades designed to protect investors against defaults, but, again, no one really knew what they did . . . except Great Cheaters. (Frankly, investors should've known. The words "default"—i.e., failure—and "swap"—i.e., trading beads for Manhattan—are right in the name.) Regardless, cheaters made money trading these. Some even realized that they could use credit default swaps to manipulate market expectations.* The more the swaps swapped, the lower a stock's price, so short sellers (clever bastards who bet that a company will fail) could make a fortune. Not only could they, but they did. Screw the rest of the world.

> **In$piration:** *"The (financial) technology got ahead of our ability to use it in responsible ways."*
> —Andrew Lo, MIT professor and bearer of good news**

Using technology to advance self-interest is what all the coolest comic book villains and richest Great Cheaters always do.

Wall Street banks withheld information about the risks of these investments from both investors and rating agencies. They made a bad loan, then passed it off to someone else, who might not have known what was up, who passed it along to someone else who didn't know, et cetera, et cetera. Local banks sold mortgages to financial institutions, who sold them to investment banks, who sold them to investors, and they scammed two friends, and they scammed two friends, and so on, and so on . . . Who knows? Maybe some of these last investors were homeowners who took out a line of credit on their unaffordable property to buy into the hot stock market, which was based on their unaffordable property! Ahh, the old circle of cheat.

---

\* You guessed it! See Chapter 24.
\*\* Steve Lohr, "In Modeling Risk, the Human Factor Was Left Out," *The New York Times,* November 5, 2008.

# The Financial Crisis

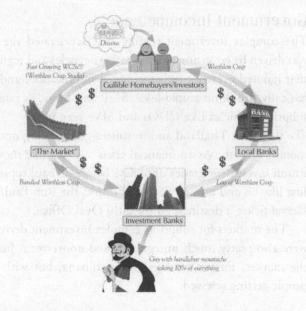

It was like an expensive game of Telephone, where the message starts as "You'll get rich," but ends up sounding like "You're screwed and I got rich!"

*Caveat suckator.* Sucker beware.

Once the collapse began, Great Cheaters used information control to keep lining their pockets. Bear Stearns's investors didn't know the company was imploding, so its CEO kept getting rich off their money. Same basic thing with Lehman, AIG, Fannie, and Freddie. Profiting from information leverage? *Shocking!* Next thing you know, we'll hear boxing is fixed and Santa Claus is not only not real, but just a ploy to keep naughty children in line. *Damn you, unforeseeable news!*

269

# Government Incompetence*

The complex investment trading that accelerated the crisis was driven by government bond rating agencies and regulators that ignored evidence, misinterpreted information, and were basically drunk on stupid-juice. S&P and Moody's rated the subprime vehicles like CDOs and SIVs very highly . . . Just like they gave Thailand an investment-grade rating until five months *after* the Asian financial crisis . . . Just like they gave Enron investment grades until days before its bankruptcy . . . Just like on and on . . . S&P still thinks the Ron Paul/Mike Gravel ticket is destined for the 2010 Oval Office.

The markets for subprime complex investment derivatives were also pretty much unregulated and unoverseen. Just like the markets for sex workers and marijuana, but with more people getting screwed.

> **In$piration:** *"The last six months have made it abundantly clear that voluntary regulation does not work."*
> —SEC chair Christopher Cox,** earning himself the 2008 Duh! Award for Excellence in Financial Obviousness

Many bankers also preyed on uneducated and unsophisticated local governments, promising to ease taxpayer demands and increase their municipal budgets with bond deals, debt trades, and swaps. Hard-hit localities ranged from New

---

\* Go looky look at Chapter 17.
\*\* Stephen Labton, "S.E.C. Concedes Oversight Flaws Fueled Collapse," *The New York Times*, September 27, 2008.

York City to the you-should-run-a-crazy-scam-there city of Birmingham, Alabama.* Hey, every town needs an adequate supply of snake oil, and there were plenty of Great Cheaters willing to be salesmen.

## Government Connections**

Of course, it wasn't just Uncle Sam's incompetence that helped so many Get Rich Cheating during the crisis, it was also his complicity. Consider Sam's distant cousins Freddie Mac and Fannie Mae. Although they sound like 1920s gangsters, they're actually highly complex independent entities and publicly traded companies, but both benefited from having the mystique of the "full faith and credit" of dear old Uncle Sam. They used that to bolster their credibility, get lower interest rates on their money supply, squeeze out competition, and generally make their lives easier and more profitable. Freddie's ability to exploit its quasi-governmental status and political ties was the key reason why former CEO Franklin Raines restated billions in losses but still made millions in bonuses. Another Freddie CEO, Richard Syron, and Fannie CEO Daniel Mudd each got over $14 million in "performance-based" pay in 2007, and then, after being given the boot for causing all sorts of problems, got more than $9 million in retirement and severance packages. Silly names, sick money.

---

* Kyle Whitmire and Mary Williams Walsh, "High Finance Backfires on Alabama County," *The New York Times*, March 12, 2008.
** Chapter 19 calling.

Fannie and Freddie earned Uncle Sam's support by doling out almost $200 million in campaign donations and lobbyist fees. John McCain's campaign manager Rick Davis got about $45,000 per month from Fannie and Freddie almost up to Election Day in 2008. The companies were so connected, many congressmen simply refused to bring regulation votes to the floor, thus sparing everyone much unpleasantness.

Of course, Fannie and Freddie were not alone among those benefiting from the crisis. Plenty of companies—from commercial banks to investment houses and insurance companies—had Uncle Sam's ear. Heck, Countrywide Financial CEO Angelo Mozilo even had a VIP list called "Friends of Angelo," for those he really liked. The list included Senators Dodd and Conrad, who helped pass emergency mortgage legislation and, gosh, got themselves some pretty decent mortgages rates to boot. *Friends don't let friends take a 6 percent, thirty-year fixed rate loan.*

## Oops, My Bad*

Ah, the do-over. So nice. As of this writing, the government has spent at least $29 billion to bail out Bear Stearns, $150 billion to shore up AIG, $135 billion to give taxpayers an economic stimulus, $200 billion to bail out Freddie and Fannie, $300 billion-ish to help out Citibank, $850 billion to bail out vague notions of bad debt, and who knows what else. Sure, Lehman Brothers "collapsed," but that was really

---

* Did someone ask for a reference to Chapter 18?

just for show. CEO Richard Fuld still made nearly half a billion dollars. Auto company CEOs lined up like Three Stooges who fly private jets to beg Congress for money. All these companies simply made themselves so indispensable that the government *had* to bail them out. They couldn't let them fail or the world would fall apart. They managed to get the United States government to take over their businesses, turning the beacon of capitalism into cheater-based socialism!

## Timing and Attitude[*]

As we learned in Part I, it's a great time to cheat. As the crisis grew, everyone looked the other way because they were all getting wealthy. Homeowners, bankers, investors, congressmen. They lived in big houses, watched plasma TVs, drove Hummers to the PTA. No one cared.

A special tip of the cheater's cap to the attitudes displayed by the Great Cheaters involved. Arrogance and entitlement work. Just days after getting an $85 billion bailout (and moments after reading Chapter 8: Your Cheatin' Heart), AIG executives arrogantly went on a ritzy $440,000 California spa retreat . . . then asked for another $38 billion line of credit. *Hey, cheating is stressful; relaxation is needed. Besides, $85 billion isn't going to spend itself, you know.*

---

[*]    Chapter 2, Chapter 4, Chapter 6, Chapter 8: Who do we appreciate? Cheaters! Cheaters! Yaaaay!

# Late to the Party?

First of all, don't worry. Experts agree that any "reforms" this crisis generates are unlikely to significantly change the massive executive pay you can get.* CEOs might make a few million less, but it's just lip service. Give the fury a little time to settle and let everyone get distracted by baseball and beaches, and it will all return to normal.

Second, the U.S. government alone has committed at least $1.5 *trillion* in loans and investments to solve the financial crisis. Lotta money getting thrown around. Lotta opportunity to cheat. All that money's gotta go somewhere and—because they're the only ones experienced in these matters—most of it will probably go to the same Great Cheaters who helped create the mess in the first place. Maybe you should get some of it too.

---

* Reed Abelson, "Banks' Bailout Unlikely to Crimp Executive Pay," *The New York Times*, October 15, 2008.

# Part III

# What If You're Caught?

## 27

# Be Prepared

## Boy Scout Planning for Nazi Youth Cheating

Even if you follow all of the advice I've just given you—make that *especially* if you follow this advice—there's a *sliiiiight* chance you might get caught. Say, oh, 95 percent. *Outside possibility*. What then? How do you prepare, what do you say, whom do you bribe?

All right, aspiring cheat, it's time to be honest with yourself (just don't let it become a habit). You've cheated your way to millions, but you're not done. You might think with the convictions of Marion Jones, Bernie Ebbers, White Oprah, and the like, everyone would believe cheating was no more. Unfortunately . . . *no*. There will still be those who think what you've done is wrong; there will be those who still don't understand that cheating is good; there will be those who want you punished; and there will be those who come after you. If you've cheated rich enough, there will be lots and lots and lots of *those*.

Great Cheaters recognize that they might get caught. I know you don't want to think about it—*frankly, I don't want to write about it*—because it's unpleasant, it's unfair, it's totally gross. But you need to grit your teeth and get through this. It'll be quick and painless, like scalp replacement surgery. Then you'll be prepared to get off. Once you've gotten off, you can lie back and see your persecution was just a minor hurdle on your path to riches beyond compare.

## Innovate
Stay ahead of the authorities. If you're motivated enough, you'll always make the technological breakthroughs first, from drug masking to electronic voting, spy cams, and fabricated accounting terms. *Keep thinking to keep cheating.*

## Overwhelm
Do lots and lots and lots and lots of things wrong. Heck, do everything in this book. Fraud, bribery, 'roids, casting couches, extortion, pillaging, murder, eating babies. It will overwhelm investigators, who'll lose track of who did what to whom when and they'll overlook certain things.

## Zip It
Don't talk to anyone who might spill the beans, whether it's your housekeeper or any other "little people." Don't let people know what you're up to. You've only got so much hush money. On a similar note, don't record yourself rejoicing in Grandma's despair—*big mistake, Enron*—or ask for bribes

when you know the Feds are listening—*you should know better, Blago's hair.*

## Destroy the Evidence

The CIA "accidentally" damaged fifty-two videotapes of its interrogation techniques and got away with their cheating. Nikolay Davydenko was cleared of fixing tennis matches after investigators were unable to review destroyed phone records. Roger Clemens, on the other hand, did *not* dispose of his evidence when trainer Brian McNamee produced seven- to ten-year-old syringes and gauze . . . *ew* . . . it was icky all around.

Get reliable document shredders. Arthur Andersen made sure their machines were top quality because they had to use them with . . . well, just about everything Andersen did involved shredding documents. Hey, it's the environmentally responsible way to *Keep* Rich Cheating.

Of course, there's also "human evidence" to destroy, with murder, suicide, and "suicide." Vito and Tony know what I'm talking about. Vince Foster—Bill and Hillary Clinton's "friend"—went bye-bye, Charles Riechers—former Air Force procurement officer with ties to the Bush White House—took the self-made exit, and just before bodybuilder David Jacobs was to provide the NFL with names of players he gave steroids to, *whoops,* he was found dead. If someone with dirt on you passes away, do send the family flowers. It's the considerate thing to do, and you can get rid of them too if the bouquet is infested with killer bees.

## E-mail Etiquette

Feast or famine. Famine is best: Don't e-mail anything. Leave no trace of your ill deeds. Follow the simple rule: *Shhhhhh, don't speak.* Eli Lilly's John C. Lechleiter wrote an e-mail in 2003 promoting the schizophrenia drug Zyprexa for off-label use—even though it caused diabetes, weight gain, and cholesterol problems. That came back to bite him later . . . giving him diabetes . . . *of the wallet.*

If you *must* e-mail, write billions, all cluttered with words like "cheat" and "guilt" and "here's the evidence you're looking for." *Why?* Most litigation involves hundreds of attorneys sifting through e-mail for tiny shreds of evidence. Since these attorneys are usually bottom-of-the-barrel, don't-wanna-be-there twentysomethings in a chemical-dependency program—*trust me, I've been one of them*—it takes a long time, costs *mucho dinero*, and will inspire the other side to drop the investigation.

## Put Things in Someone Else's Name

Every transaction must go through an intermediary. Never sign for your FedEx of anabolic steroids, Botox, stolen script, or competitor's secret recipe. That's what interns and vice presidents are for.

## Build Support

Fan clubs, a party base, invested donors, constituents, baby mommas . . . these people will defend you no matter what your crime. You could also breed defenders, like Frank Quattrone,* who started "The Innocence Project" at Santa Clara Law School. Daring: He was humble enough to think he'd need the Innocence Project *and* arrogant enough to name it something so obvious and self-serving.

Are you two-faced enough to be both humble and arrogant? You'd better say yes, unless you want to Get *Caught* Cheating.

## CC: The Pope, Joe Biden, et al.

Put the following at the bottom of every memo that you write: "cc: U.S. Department of Justice and local clergy." *Don't actually send a copy*, but now you've got the whole "I've got nothing to hide; I was very forthright throughout; why would I tell everyone about it if it was wrong?" thing down.

## Buy Now!

Things starting to heat up to the point where your PR hacks need to hire PR hacks to deflect all the bad news? Flip ahead to Chapter 30's discussion of countries without extradition treaties. Buy a house in one of those places now. Establishing residency will help speed your escape. If you wait until you're on the lam, real estate brokers will take advantage of your desperation . . . and make you take out a—*gasp!*—subprime mortgage.

---

* Quattrone, the former head of CSFB, was charged with both using lucrative shares and tips in IPOs to get business for his firm and pressuring analysts to write favorable reports for his clients, *i.e., being smart.*

## Meet Your Family

Introduce yourself to your kids, shake hands with your wife, leave your mistress in the car. At some point, you're going to want to resign "to spend more time with your family."*

## Lawyers, Cons, and Money

When they're not overbilling you, lawyers are actually useful, if you have good ones. *Why?*

- They know every rule to break, every loophole through which to jump, every incriminating document to be labeled "attorney-client privilege."
- They'll do anything for money. *Anything.*
- Big law firms, with their intertwined clients, have their own conflicts of interest. Therefore, covering up your misdeeds will help them cover up their own. That's a nice "convergence of interest."
- Having a lawyer sign off on your actions gives you someone else to blame and helps you deny wrongdoing. Always nice.
- Anyone who can say, "If the glove don't fit, you must acquit," with a straight face must have Great Cheater blood.
- They usually defend murderers and rapists. You'll be a slight upgrade.
- Lawyers are a great source of information about their

---

* Source: Every retiring cheater ever. Ever. *Ever.*

other clients. If you can't pry some useful nuggets of knowledge from them with wine or women, remember: They'll do anything for money. *Anything*.

- The best lawyers are trained, first and foremost, to overwhelm and delay, to make you look reasonable, and to allow the guiltiest criminal to walk free on the most technical of technicalities. Just like the good Cheating Lord intended.

As a Great Cheater, you can afford to hire the top legal minds, the best private investigators, the most soulless of publicists. Doing this won't just level the playing field, it'll tip it all the way in your favor. Opposing attorneys and investigators know their every move will be publicly scrutinized, and the prospect of being second-guessed will throw them off their game. Then you'll win.

How do I know all this? Trust me . . . I'm a you-know-what.

## Corral the Pigs, Fry the Bacon

Most anti-cheating authorities lack the resources, energy, time, motivation, and ability to pursue geniuses like you. Nonetheless, some delusional crusaders may persist because they've watched too many reruns of *The Untouchables*. It's up to you, Almost Great Cheater, to eliminate them. For the good of the country. For the good of the world. For the good of *you*.

Knock down those who would knock you down. Take out the legal losers trying to play by the rules. It's been done before.

- William Lerach (whose smug, worthless Milberg Weiss law firm got $7.2 billion from Enron) was indicted in kickback schemes. *Not soon enough.*
- Richard "Dickie" Scruggs (the anti-American pioneer of tobacco and asbestos litigation and inspiration for Russell Crowe's character in *The Insider**) was convicted of low-level bribery. *Because being a lame buzzkill is not yet a crime.*
- Before his bust for being Emperor's Club Client Number 9, Eliot Spitzer spent years harassing noble Great Cheaters just to get back at his parents for naming him "Eliot." *So you got picked last for kickball. Get over it.*

Those do-gooders were taken out by seemingly random scandals. Spitzer resigned after he was caught in a prostitution ring, part of an unrelated record sweep in a tax inquiry, just like Bill Clinton's impeachment started in a real estate investigation. *Were these setups?* Probably not. *Will they inspire setups in the future?* Maybe, maybe not. I'm not saying you should entrap your enemies, but I'm also not saying you shouldn't unentrap them.

Unfortunately, that doesn't cover everyone. There are still misguided officials who can't be bought or caught, who actually believe it's their *duty* to pursue corruption, fraud, political

---

* He should be jailed just for keeping that drunk Aussie's career alive.

improprieties, steroids, bribery, and other great stuff.* *What a bunch of jerks.*

Negate their power. Try these ideas.

1. Have higher-up authorities restrict, even punish, them. Carol Lam led the corruption prosecution against Randall "Duke" Cunningham, and was, *shockingly,* fired by Alberto Gonzales in January 2007. *Gracias, Alberto.*

2. Most prosecutors have grand political aspirations. Donate to their campaigns. *Repeatedly.*

3. If all else fails, write letters to shame him or her out of office. Here's a template:

*Dear [pain-in-the-butt's name here]:*

    *I don't like you. Nobody likes you. You need to focus on important crimes, like jaywalking and pot smoking. Stop needlessly harassing hard-working CEOs, team owners, and studio executives, you political hack. I hope you rot in hell.*

    *Your enemy forever and Ever and EVER,*
    *[Your name]*


*P.S. Enclosed please find a donation for your reelection campaign. You'll remember me, won't you?*

---

* Like California's Bill Lockyer—who even filed a suit against the six biggest automakers *for global warming.*

## 28

## Deny, Deny, Deny

### Blame the Underlings

Stave off prosecution as long as possible. You don't want your assets frozen before you escape in the middle of the night. According to pop psychologists, there are five stages of grief: Denial, Anger, Bargaining, Depression, and Acceptance. These can all be applied to the grief of Getting Caught Getting Rich Cheating.

```
    DENIAL:    "I don't know what you're talking
               about and I didn't do it."


     ANGER:    "I said, I Didn't Do It!!"


 BARGAINING:   "Oh, come onnnnn . . ."


 DEPRESSION:   "I'm upset you'd even think I did
               it."


 ACCEPTANCE:   "It was Johnson!"
```

# Deny, Deny, Deny

There are two styles of denial:

1. *Angry.* Rafael Palmeiro adamantly wagged his finger at a congressional committee and insisted, "I have never used steroids. Period. I don't know how to say it any more clearly than that. Never." That was a mere five months before testing positive. Roger Clemens released an online video denial, went on *60 Minutes*, filed a defamation suit, taped phone calls, held press conferences, and smashed a tiny crippled boy against his forehead. Bill Clinton hissed that he "did not have sex with *that* woman." He was pointing to a reporter from the *Times-Ledger* when he said "that woman," so, technically, he was telling the truth.

2. *Vague.* An elusive denial gives you the wiggle room to say you meant whatever is convenient to have meant later. Barry Bonds said he never *knowingly* took steroids, Jerome Kerviel at Société Générale said he'd made a mistake and would "fix it," Sacred Heart University "is not necessarily aware of donations" from lenders that might be inducements,* and Captain Renault was "shocked—shocked—to find that gambling is going on" as he gathered his winnings at Rick's Café.

---

* Jonathan D. Glater, "New Ties Found to Link Lenders to Colleges," *The New York Times,* September 5, 2007.

## Plausible Deniability

If you had *no idea* that something bad was going on, surely you can't get in trouble for it. *Riiiiiight?* This unique form of denial will work for you. *I guarantee it!*[*]

You'll need to tell investigators things like "I didn't know about that," "It was beyond the scope of my knowledge," "I never authorized such a thing," "It was my first day," and "Who are you, and how did you get into my office?" To make these claims possible, you must start building circumstantial evidence that you were, in fact, out of the loop, absent, or simply "eccentric" (the rich-people word for "crazy").

**CHEAT CHAT**

Brains for Dummies

• • • • • • • • • • • • • • • • • • • • • • • • • • • • •

One of the great ironies of Getting Rich Cheating is that you must appear incompetent to be innocent of actions that required great intelligence. Dummies just don't fraud their way to millions. It takes cunning, innovation, and a sharp mind.

"But what if I'm actually *not* very smart?"

Well, it'll be easy to establish plausible deniability, won't it, George W. Bush?

---

[*] Still not a guarantee.

Whether you're a genius or moron, follow Great Cheaters' examples to establish that you're "plausibly denied," i.e., a loon:

- Each day, designate one lucky worker to be the starburst in your name (Walmart).
- Videotape yourself, um, doing, uh, "inappropriate things" with underage girls . . . (R. Kelly).
- . . . or boys (M. Jackson).
- Make your family drama public news (the Osbournes, Spearses, and Trumps, et cetera).
- Name illegal transactions after *Star Wars* characters (Enron).
- Be Howard Hughes (Howard Hughes).
- Marry Anna Nicole Smith (various).

## Deny Everything
Over and over and over and over and over and over and over again.

- Repeat something enough times, eventually it becomes true.
- Repeat something enough times, eventually it becomes true.
- Repeat something enough times, eventually . . .

## Blame Everyone
If your enemies don't believe your denials, start pointing fingers. All the Great Cheaters have. Hewlett-Packard's Pa-

tricia Dunn blamed junior execs for the pretexting *she herself ordered.** Juiced ballplayers blame wives, trainers, nannies, agents, and deals with the Devil, a.k.a. George Steinbrenner. Maurice Greenberg actually sued his AIG employees for $1.46 billion to cover a regulatory fine. Lehman's Richard Fuld blamed the media, short sellers, the government, and a run on the bank, and Ken Lay blamed everybody from Skilling to Fastow to Arthur Andersen, the *Wall Street Journal*, short sellers, and a "witch hunt" . . . which does explain why federal prosecutor Sean Berkowitz turned into a newt. (Berkowitz did, in fact, get "bettah."**)

Besides those working beneath you, who and what else can you blame? Here are some popular scapegoats of the past few years:

- Alcoholism
- Hurricane Katrina
- 9/11
- Childhood abuse
- OxyContin
- Sarbanes-Oxley
- "Competition"
- The Senior Vice President of Scapegoating

---

* Much to my surprise, pretexting is neither reading a speech before it's delivered nor traveling into the past to prevent yourself from drunk-messaging that girl at three a.m.

** *Monty Python and the Holy Grail,* directed by Terry Gilliam and Terry Jones (1975).

- Osama bin Laden
- The BCS (Bowl Championship Series) computer rankings

## Spin Out of Trouble

Quality spin won't just help you Get Rich Cheating, it could help you Stay Out of Jail Cheating. It controls the damage of an accusation long enough for the news cycle to leap away to some starlet's affair with Owen Wilson or for you to get your yacht to international waters. Let the Great Cheaters lead the way again.

**In$piration:** *"I misremembered."* —**Roger Clemens**

Roger Clemens wasn't injecting steroids, he was, uh, injecting the anesthetic lidocaine and vitamin $B_{12}$! Sure, because everyone takes vitamins through the butt. Everyone cool, that is.

**In$piration:** *"When the president does it, that means it's not illegal."*

—**Richard Milhous Nixon on phone tapping**

Aren't you the victim of a "vast right-wing conspiracy" just like Bill and Hillary Clinton?

**In$piration:** *"I don't recall."*

—**Attorney General Alberto Gonzales explaining why prosecutors were fired**

# Get Rich Cheating

It was hard work that did it, not cheating.

**In$piration:** *"I never asked."*
>                    —Barry Bonds on accidental use of PEDs

Childhood trauma. That's always a good excuse.

**In$piration:** *"Wasn't mine."*
>                    —Tom Sizemore after being found with a prosthetic penis
>                    filled with urine for a drug test

You have a chemical addiction and need rehab, right Mel Gibson, Mark Foley, and everyone who lives in Los Angeles?

**In$piration:** *"Scott, we now know, is disgruntled about his experience at the White House. For those of us who fully supported him, before, during, and after he was press secretary, we are puzzled. It is sad—this is not the Scott we knew."*
>                    —Dana Perino explaining away Scott McClellan's
>                    book divulging White House cheating

Representative William Jefferson—who hid money in his freezer—told a judge his deeds were technically more akin to "influence peddling" than bribery . . . because peddlers don't lose their elected office.

**In$piration:** *"I misinterpreted the rules."*

—Bill Belichick

Microsoft's attorneys claimed that the company's bundling of Explorer and Windows wasn't monopolistic, but rather "innovative." Nice. You know who else was innovative? Stalin.

**In$piration:** *"Vanishing twin."*

—Tyler Hamilton explaining why he had two types of blood in his system

Sometimes, girls will "just be girls," right, Lindsay, Paris, and Britney? No harm done . . . or at least, not much.

**In$piration:** *"Depends upon what your definition of 'is' is."* —Bill Clinton, still smiling

And, of course, old reliable human nature.

**Succes$tory:** *"The snake made me do it."* —Eve

## Cover Carefully

Senator Ted Stevens was convicted on seven felony counts because he didn't disclose $250,000 in renovations from Bill Allen's company; associates of Jack Abramoff got nailed because they didn't report the gifts they arranged between congressmen and clients; Martha Stewart got in trouble for not coming clean about stock sale info. Look, cheater, just be careful when you lie.

> **Le$$on:** *A transaction is rarely the criminal act in corporate or political crime. It's usually the cover-up of the transaction, right, White Oprah?*

## Investigate Yourself

So you haven't denied your way out of trouble yet? What's a "good citizen" like you to do? Like the Great Cheaters before you, simply investigate yourself. *Nudge, wink, rrrrow.*

Ever get pulled over for a speeding ticket and the officer says, "Any idea how fast you were going?" You could just reply, "No, but I'll look into it. I'll just let myself off with a warning. Thanks." Then drive off. Investigating yourself is just like that.

> **In$piration:** *"We hear there's something wrong. Don't worry. We're looking into it. Go about the business of ignoring our business. We've got it covered."*
>
> —You

Don't think Great Cheaters "investigate themselves"?* Well, in recent years the NBA, NHL, NFL, MLB, and Women's Tennis Association have "investigated" the cheats of

---

* "Investigate yourself" sounds like something you'd normally pay a dominatrix to do, right? *Right?*

steroids, gambling, and too many beautiful Russian women. Also looking into their own cheating are Obama's White House, the Pentagon, the State Department, Representative Charles Rangel, the U.S. Congress, the College Board, Hewlett-Packard, Auburn University, and that creepy guy at the YMCA showers. The members of the public don't pay attention to *who does* the investigating, they just hear there's been an investigation and that's fine with them.

How do you investigate yourself?[*]

*You don't.* It's costly and you might find something wrong. If you must, then just *pretend* to do so. Refuse to be interviewed, like Karl Rove, Harriet Miers, and Sarah Palin. Form a committee, task them with investigation, have the members take in a movie, pocket their million-dollar budget, and call it a day. Go have a drink, say something inappropriate to a woman, have her killed before she can report it, hire three illegal immigrants to say you were with them as an alibi, turn them in to INS and have them killed, then call *that* a night. Wash. Rinse. Repeat. In other words, "Don't."

Of course, you'll want to make it look like you did a thorough investigation. So get a nice three-ring binder and write up a "report." (Make sure it's dated *after* the start of the alleged investigation. Don't just pull an old "I'm innocent" out of the file cabinet: If you submit a "2009 Report on Doing Nothing Wrong" dated 1976, you'll have lots of 'splaining to do.)

Your fake report should obviously absolve you of any

---

[*]   Candlelight and Barry White sets a nice mood.

cheating and preclude further investigation, like in the cases of these Great Cheaters:

- Merck behaved "more or less perfectly" in handling the Vioxx drug—which injured thousands—according to an investigator *hired by the company.*

- Major League Baseball's Mitchell Report didn't find as much PED use as is generally believed to exist and gave weak recommendations with the sole purpose of dissuading outside inquiry. *Come on, who's got time for snitching? The game is on!*

- Al Gore led an inquiry into Apple Computer's options practices and—despite some backdating and "suspicious activity"—found nothing wrong. You know, Al Gore, the guy on Apple's board of directors. *That's an Inconvenient Truth.*

- The Consumer Product Safety Commission found "no instances of hazardous levels" in vinyl lunch boxes, even though they actually found one in five contained dangerous amounts of lead. *According to the Cheaters English Dictionary, "No instances" means "Don't make a big deal about it."*

In similarly unbiased findings, Donald Rumsfeld said he did a great job, Paris Hilton claims her album is "totally, like, hot," and Yogi Bear insists he didn't steal any pic-a-nic baskets. *Hey, Boo-Boo, we've got a con-fa-lict of interest.*

What if you actually find something wrong?

*Shut up, shut up, shut up!* Okay, fine, you found something "wrong." Weigh the cost of fixing the problem against your bottom line; then ignore the results.

- The NFL destroyed the evidence against the New England Patriots, closed the case, and moderately punished Bill Belichick, long before Spygate had truly run its course. *Touchdown for cheater!*
- Guidant covered up years of internal documents showing the dangers of its heart stents and defibrillators, just long enough to be bought for $27 billion by Boston Scientific. *Who knew exploding hearts made the sound "cha-ching"?*
- The Education Department brushed aside a finding by its own inspector that a student lender—Pennsylvania Higher Education Assistance Agency—improperly received $34 million in federal subsidies . . . then it told the lender to decide for itself how much to pay back. *Hey, kid, you done bad, so either go to your room or eat a bottomless bowl of ice cream.*

In other words, cover it up and punish yourself.* Fly yourself to an island. Sit in the corner. Think about what you've done. Bad boy. Very, very bad boy.**

Now go help OJ find the real killers.

---

\* Still sounds kinky. Do I need to take a cold shower?
\** Ibid.

# 29

# Hearings and Trials

## Swear to Cheat the Truth, the Whole Truth, and Nothing But the Truth

Weak, poor people fear words like "hearing" and "trial" because they're losers. You should see these as opportunities to prove your cheating mettle. It's one thing to trick employees, shareholders, and customers—it's quite another to undermisrepresentimate in a room filled with those with the power to put you in jail or, worse, take away your money.

## Congressional Hearings

When denial and self-investigation can't quell the rising furor against you, you may be called to testify before the United States Congress. Considering other regular testifiers—the MLB, oil companies, the pharmaceutical industry, cigarette makers, Oliver North—you're in great company. *Check that*, you're in Great Cheater company.

Congressional hearings are different than trials. Trials

usually just involve a few broken promises, maybe a dead kid who took steroids because of you, a comatose patient or two. No big deal. A congressional hearing, on the other hand, means your success has become a matter of national importance. *Congratulations, you must've cheated yourself quite rich.*

Don't worry: Elected officials know the importance of wealth, social status, and cheating, so they'll be sympathetic to someone of your stature. The congressional hearing is merely a venue for disclosure without disclosing anything, a place to testify and say nothing, the least effective, most public wrist slap in the world.

> **Le$$on:** *Don't piss off Pennsylvania Senator Arlen Spector. He likes showboating and will call a hearing just because his Eagles lost to the Patriots.*

No one respects Congress, not even congressmen themselves. It's a circus designed solely to distract constituents from noticing that their representatives do nothing useful at all. Enjoy your star turn in the center ring.

Your congressional hearing goals: Admit nothing, make future bribery contacts, and convince Congress to allow, even encourage, everything you've done and plan to do, without acknowledging you've done or plan to do anything at all.

### Great Cheaters Hearing Tip #1: Prepare

Hire a good testimony coach: Blackwater CEO Erik Prince had former Hillary Clinton advisor Mark Penn teach him how to admit nothing. Old buddy Clemens, believing he could brush back senators like a rookie pinch hitter, visited nineteen of forty members of the committee he was to testify before, signing autographs, taking pictures, and suggesting he'd rip off their heads with his mind.

### Great Cheaters Hearing Tip #2: Own the Committee

Larry Sonsini represented Hewlett-Packard in testimony before Congress before a committee that was plumb full of lawmakers to whose campaigns his firm had generously contributed. *I'm sure that helped just a little.*

### Great Cheaters Hearing Tip #3: Neither Swear Nor Be Sworn

When executives from the major oil companies testified before Congress in 2006 regarding excessive profits, they were not required to swear they were telling the truth. This is tremendous help for Tip #7 below.

### Great Cheaters Hearing Tip #4: It's Visual

These hearings are all for show to entertain constituents back home with a two-second clip on the news or a photo in the paper. To that end, remember, a picture is worth a thousand words.* So get the picture right. You want sympathy, empathy, understanding, compassion, and love.

- Wear an American flag pin.
- Look contrite.
- Have your "wife" (or an attractive actress playing the same) sit behind you. When you're questioned, she should fan herself, whimper, rub rosary beads, cry, faint. Note: Long hair is "trampy."
- Your "mom" would be a good addition too.
- Kids? Sure, as long as they're cute, in a wheelchair, or afflicted with whooping cough.
- Have the ridiculous CODEPINK demonstrate against you. Their antics are so absurd, people automatically side *against* them and thus *with* you.
- Don't forget the story about how your father was just a hard-working milkman/miner/cobbler who wanted a better life for everyone.
- Start every answer with, "Senator, since I love freedom more than I love myself . . ."
- Do not be a minority or woman.

## Great Cheaters Hearing Tip #The Fifth: Speak No Evil

You "plead the Fifth" when you refuse to testify under oath on the grounds that your answers could be used against you. It's from the Fifth Amendment to the Constitution, designed

---

* Of course, if you had your hands on the picture, you'd claim it was a priceless heirloom and sell it for fifteen thousand words.

to prevent government abuse by the King of England. Obviously, it should be used to avoid admitting that you Got Rich Cheating. Plead the Fifth to all questions you're asked. Do it. Everyone does.*

## Great Cheaters Hearing Tip #6: Evade
The 2005 congressional hearings on steroids in baseball offered a hard-hitting lineup of diverse and varied evasion. Mark McGwire said he didn't want to talk about the past, Sammy Sosa claimed he couldn't speak English,** Rafael Palmeiro pointed and yelled, and Jose Canseco sold Representative Henry Waxman a month's supply of Rogaine.

## Great Cheaters Hearing Tip #7: Lie
Worried about lying "under oath" or after putting your hand on a Bible? Come on, if you believed in a greater power who'd punish you for deceit, would you even be here now, or would you be a pillar of salt?

# On Trial in Style
If your congressional hearing goes poorly or doesn't go at all, you may find yourself heading to court. You're on trial for Getting Rich Cheating. Don't worry—*a lot* of Great Cheaters have been there. Let them show you how to fight.

---

* Everyone. Really.
** The "no speaky English" defense is popular. Charles Rangel said he failed to report $75,000 in rental income because of "cultural and language barriers" even though many of his constituents speak only Spanish.

## Great Cheaters Trial Tip #1: Hearts and Mind Control

Celebrities have it easy when they go on trial. Well-known celebri-criminals like Winona Ryder, Kiefer Sutherland, and OJ Simpson hypnotize starstruck jurors and judges, in whose eyes they're gods. If you've cheated your way into fame, there will be no juror able to treat you like a regular criminal. If you give their lives enough meaning, surely they won't be mean enough to give you life.

Less famous Great Cheaters need to work harder to influence public opinion. Learn from HealthSouth's Richard Scrushy, who read the Bible on a morning TV show called *Viewpoint* in Birmingham during his trial and had his own show called *Amen Corner*. A regular preacher on that show was paid by Scrushy to have local black pastors support him. Scrushy himself preached in churches and invited folks to his trial. Just in case piety wasn't enough, he also paid a reporter, Audry Lewis, thousands of dollars to write favorable articles about him in the *Birmingham Times*, and his son-in-law bought two local TV stations in the area. Pretty solid ratings for *The Richard Scrushy Is Innocent Hour* or *The Richard Scrushy Will Pay Jurors One Million Dollars to Acquit Him Jamboree*.

## Great Cheaters Trial Tip #2: Dress the Part

Hollywood cheaters know all about looking fine to distract the press and jurors. If you've cheated in another field, call up your stylist friends to make you look suitably attractive (Lindsay Lohan) or insane (Nick Nolte), depending upon your defense plans.

## Great Cheaters Trial Tip #3: Discover This!

The discovery process is a wonderful *pretrial* way to both delay judgment and obscure the truth. We already discussed creating fake e-mails to throw off litigation teams. What about just piling up the evidence so it overwhelms all parties? The defendants in a fraud case related to Hollinger CFO John Boultbee asked a Chicago judge for a postponement because they couldn't possibly review "the mountains of paperwork in time."* *Make mountains out of your cheating molehills.*

## Great Cheaters Trial Tip #4: Own the Court

One great thing about America is that judges are often elected. Campaign contributions tend to outweigh judicial philosophy.**

Enlist old friends, bribery, and blackmail. Start with the judges, move to the prosecutors, jury, witnesses, and court reporters. Justice may be blind, but she's still gotta pay the rent, and those scales register gold.

## Great Cheaters Trial Tip #5: Take Advantage of Procedural Loopholes

Represent yourself, like old pal Anthony Pellicano. They say a man who is his own lawyer has a fool for a client, but that'd nicely set up your insanity defense, eh? Or claim immunity. Are you a telecommunications company accused of helping

---

\*  *The New York Post*, January 9, 2007.

\*\* According to a study by some eggheads (Adam Lipt, "Looking Anew at Campaign Cash and Elected Judges," *The New York Times*, January 29, 2008), contributors got favorable rulings about 65 to 80 percent of the time.

the government cheat by spying? Well, never mind, you're free to go.

Use new, poorly understood laws to your advantage. Recent Supreme Court rulings have "raised the bar for aggrieved shareholders, requiring them to provide more detailed evidence of wrongdoing when they sue, before the discovery phase, when lawyers have a chance to gather information."* Translation: It's harder to be sued for corporate cheating.

Object. Annoying legal objections are a Great Cheater's best friend. Grab a trial prep book and start yelling. *Hearsay! Circumstantial evidence! The statute of limitations has run out! Motion to dismiss! Motion to reconsider! It's not the size of the legal defense but the motion of the ocean!*

The more you can slow down the process, the better. It'll take up the court's time, confuse sleepy and annoyed jurors, and delay incarceration until your political friends can pardon you.

## Great Cheaters Trial Tip #6: De-fense! (clap, clap) De-fense! (clap, clap)

Fortunately, cheating in politics, sports, and entertainment rarely is grounds for a court case. But that doesn't mean you can't learn a thing or ten from your brethren and their experience.

Here are some brilliant, innovative, imaginative—*but real*—legal arguments put forward by the Great Cheaters. *Will their awesomeness never stop?*

---

* Jonathan D. Glater, "Wave of Lawsuits Over Losses Could Hit a Wall," *The New York Times*, May 8, 2008.

- WorldCom CEO Bernie Ebbers claimed not to know what was going on, a move that actually became known as the "Aw, shucks" defense. *The Aw, shucks defense was, of course, pioneered in the 1957 case of Wally v. The Beaver.*

- Richard Scrushy asked a judge to throw out the case against him since his lawyers had been tricked into revealing his strategy, *which happened to have been "Get tricked into revealing my strategy; then ask the judge to throw out the case."*

- Take-Two Interactive's CEO claimed that his misdeeds were due to a back injury he had suffered while playing polo. *Polo injuries always get the sympathy of blue-collar jurors.*

- William Aramony, of United Way of America, diverted $2 million to pay for chauffeurs, apartments, and gifts for his teenage girlfriend. His attorney argued, in part, that the crimes were caused by shrinkage in the area of the brain that controls impulses and inhibitions. Shrinkage in an area of the brain. *So much more specific than pleading insanity.*

Then, of course, there was the corporate king, Enron.

- One supporter testified, "Yes, it's bad, but it's not evil," thereby establishing a new standard in American Justice: *Innocent until proven evil.*

- Attorneys labeled a prosecution witness a greedy coward acting purely in self-interest. *Isn't it true, Mr. Kettle, that, as my client Mr. Pot said, you are indeed black?*

- CEO Jeffrey Skilling said he couldn't remember the details of the board meeting when Andrew Fastow described the partnerships used to hide Enron's losses . . . because the lights went out. Really. "The lights went out." At the giant energy company. *Clever.*

- The defense had the insight to suggest that Skilling was just being *sarcastic* when he said, "they're on to us." Ah, the old "just kidding" defense from the British common law precedent of Cooties v. No-Give-Backs. *Frankly, I would've gone with a "Whoever smelt it, dealt it" strategy.*

Of course, if you get desperate, here are some original Get Rich Cheating trial techniques to gain acquittal. They'll work. Trust me, I'm sorta one of them.

- *"Patriotism is the yaddayaddayadda."* Still. Wasn't everything you did for the good of the country? Hey, there haven't been any more terrorist attacks since you started cheating, have there? No, there haven't. Don't forget that American flag pin.

- Tell a hostile witness his pants are on fire. The jury will suspect he's a liar liar.

- Claim that the *real* cheater is about to enter the court.

# Get Rich Cheating

When the jurors turn to look toward the door, tell
them that means they have a reasonable doubt.

- Every now and then, just under his breath, have your
  lawyer say to the jury, "Jurorswho'llvotetoacquitsay-
  what?" *Freedom!*

These tactics will all work. I guarantee it.*

---

* No, no, no, not a guarantee.

# 30

# When Life Gives You Lemons . . .

## . . . Make Cheater-Aid

They got ya, and things are looking grim. What's a Great Cheater to do? You can run for it, settle it, or face your sentence. Not pleasant options, but you'll survive.

## Run for It, Marty

Scrushy again. Prosecutors accused him of trying to flee the country in February '07 when he took a cruise on his yacht, *Chez Soiree*. Sir Richard said he was just going with his family on a court-approved trip to Disney World. Sure, going from Alabama to Orlando on a boat may be . . . bumpy . . . but he's not a sailor, he's a Great Cheater.

> **Le$$on:** *Ultimately, bad weather kept Scrushy from leaving the coast. Get a reliable weather tracking system for your escape yacht.*

# Know Your Extradition Treaties

Wikipedia lists countries with friendly extradition treaties. Do NOT flee to these places. I can't stress that enough. Go somewhere that the long, flabby arm of the law can't reach. Wesley Snipes and Comverse CEO Kobi Alexander fled to Namibia, and boy band cheater Lou Pearlman was found checked into a hotel in Bali under the name "A. Incognito Johnson." Really.

So go somewhere exotic and enjoy. If you need to feel power, use your real money (as opposed to their coconut-based currency) to buy yourself a dictatorship. Then build tiny replicas of your favorite worldwide cities and smash them like the rich Godzilla you are. In addition to Bali and Namibia, here are some hidden gems I suggest you quickly find on a map: Crooksburgh, the Republic of Lies, Roidsylvania, Fakeboobistan, Bribery and Herzegovina, and the Mockery Coast.

# Settle It Out

Secretly meet with prosecutors to make a deal. They don't want to go to trial any more than you do. They'll also be looking for jobs once the whole country is bankrupt, so make some "arrangements" for future employment.

Consider selling out whoever you can. Find a bigger fish for the government to fry. Bosses, friends, politicians, even your wife. Hope she really meant, "For better or worse."

Whether or not you do that, rest assured, most cheating settlements aren't even slaps on the wrist: they're just a gentle rubbing of the wrist to relieve tension. The Justice

Department has shifted away from prosecution of corporate misdeeds to fines, integrity agreements, and "monitoring" programs. So, (a) budget for a fine, and (b) budget for bribing the "monitors." An ounce of cheating prevention is worth a pound of cheating cure.

It's a nice situation for a Great Cheater: Steal ten bucks, *go to jail*. Steal $10 million, *get a monitoring deal*. Download a song, *suffer*. Download thousands of credit cards, *take a vacation*. When a Great Cheater gets caught with his hand in the cookie jar, he only has to put the cookie back, or whatever's left of it . . .

**Succes$tory:** *"We're not guilty, but, gee, if we have to agree to do basically nothing about it . . . okaaaay."*

—Everyone

 **CHEAT CHAT**
Have Lots

It's *vital* that you cheated yourself *so rich* that even a big fine doesn't dent the pile of money buried in the Swiss bank accounts and under the floorboards of your French chateau.

Plus, you ought to hide your assets. Transfer them to your family or into real estate because certain states, like Texas and Florida, don't allow seizure of homes to fulfill sentences. So if you do go to jail, you can come out to a wife with a plump bank account and a gold-plated man-

> sion. Whether you should dump her for a younger hot-
> tie who doesn't know your secrets is up to you. *Hint: You
> should.*

If you've got the cash, just settle it. Hopefully they only found a tiny portion of what you cheated, and giving up some small things will throw them off the trail of the big ones.

So say you're sorry, beg forgiveness, then go spend the *real* loot. It's not like you robbed a 7-Eleven and should go to jail, right?

# Sentencing, Schmentencing

> *"'Tis better to beg forgiveness than to ask permission."*
> —Concheatus, Confucius's brother-in-law

If you don't settle and don't escape, you'll be sentenced. This is your last chance to plead your case. Beg for mercy, call upon your family, list all your contributions to society. Heck, didn't you give investigators work, thus growing the economy? They should be thanking you . . .

Some Great Cheater sentencing pleas:

- Former Qwest CEO Joseph Nacchio's lawyer noted that he didn't sell all his stock via inside information. "If he had a corrupt heart and was intent on cheating people . . . he could have sold everything." *So, just keep a little on the side. For flaky legal argument's sake.*

- Marion Jones told the judge she lied to protect her family and asked not to be separated from her two sons, even for a minute. "I ask you to be as merciful as a human being can be," she said, crying on her husband's shoulder. *Nice touch with the fake humanity thing, Miss Speedy McRoid-a-Lot.*

- The CEO of Brocade Communications orchestrated a backdated option scandal and at his sentencing said, "I'm sorry. There is much that I regret, and if I could turn back the clock, I would." Um. That's what got you into this situation in the first place! Daringly stupid, but at least he wins the prize for world's least effective mea culpa ever. Unless Jeffrey Dahmer said, "I'm sorry. I wish I could just stab, chop, and eat all my mistakes."

## What's the Worst They Can Do?

Marion Jones had to give back her five Olympic gold medals, spend six months in jail, and do a bunch of community service. *Yawn. I can serve six months in my sleep.* Ben Johnson was stripped of his gold medal and banned from competition. *Yeah, like he wanted to run without the juice anyway.* Floyd Landis was stripped of his Tour de France title. *What's with the stripping of titles? Who cares?* They can't travel back in time and wipe your victory from the public consciousness. You still get to be famous, and that's worth at least six figures in speaker's fees.

## Jail Ain't So Bad

The Great Cheaters go to minimum security prison. You'll survive. You can actually hire a "post-conviction placement specialist" to help you choose which federal prison you'll end up in. It's worth the $50,000 to make sure you get to have nice crafts, tennis, softball, and golf.

Come on . . . It's minimum security prison with no fencing . . .

Tonight on *Oz: Great Cheaters Files,* watch tough guys play eight-ball . . . *instead of billiards!* Be shocked by caviar . . . *that's not Beluga!* Be amazed as the board of directors rows crew . . . *without a coxswain!* Tremble in your seats as thirsty diners have to drink chardonnay . . . *from Oregon!*

"Hey! Who does a COO have to downsize around here to get a sun-dried-tomato-and-pesto omelet?"

# Faking Death
If jail really isn't for you, there's one surefire way to avoid it: Fake your own death.

> **In$piration:** *"To be, or not to be: that is the question . . . To sleep, perchance to dream. Ay, there's the rub . . ."*
> —Shakespeare

> **In$piration:** *"To still get seats at Spago: Oooh, that'll be tough . . ."* —You

# 31

# Your Second Act

## How Cheater Got Her Groove Back

Even if you're punished for cheating, don't worry, you can still have a successful, happy, wealthy life. Everyone gets a second chance . . . well, at least all the Great Cheaters do. Go to rehab, write a(nother) book, start a different investing company, and "reinvent" yourself.

- Robert Downey Jr. was busted for drug and weapons charges . . . and his career actually soared, with TV roles, Golden Globes, and more. For cheat's sake, he was Iron Man! He used dirty money to build a suit of metal with which he can destroy his enemies! Art imitates life!
- George O'Leary got caught faking his resume to coach at Notre Dame and is now a high-paid NFL assistant.
- Tonya Harding whacked Nancy Kerrigan's knee and is now a sought-after celebrity wrestler and white-trash train-wreck lifestyle TV expert.

- Jason Giambi used steroids more than most use water, but because he pulled a "my bad" and owned up to his past behaviors, he's again a beloved baseball player making millions and, during one stretch of 2008, inspiring a moustache revolution.
- Every athlete is probably a cheater, and every athlete seems to have a second career in broadcasting. So there's that.
- Ted Stevens was convicted of his previously mentioned seven felonies . . . and a week later almost got reelected to the U.S. Senate.
- Michael Alix, a *risk manager at Bear Stearns*, was appointed to a senior position in the Federal Reserve because the government clearly needs to be run by someone who knows *a whole lot* about the financial crisis.
- No matter what they've done, Michael Milken is a multimillionaire consultant, Henry Blodget is a well-respected business commentator, and Don Imus will always find a place to rant and rave about the injustices put upon the white man.

## Image Is Everything . . . Still

In order to have a successful second act, you need to rehabilitate your image.

First, make a public apology that pushes all the right buttons. *Family, faith, patriotism.* Milken told stories about surviving cancer. Jimmy Swaggart and Jim Bakker made tearful confessions of their sins. Andy Pettitte quoted scripture and said, "I was desperate . . . Do I think I'm a cheater? No, from the bottom of my heart. I wish I hadn't done it. Stupid." Sure, he wishes he hadn't done it, since he was caught, but let's not get caught up in semantics. Let's get caught up in how rich he's cheating.

Second, literally change your image. The private contractor Blackwater softened its logo after getting into trouble for being opportunistic—and inspirational—war zone facilitators. Now the company is a gentle, caring—and rich—war zone facilitator.

Third, hit the talk show circuit. Larry King, Charlie Rose, Wolf Blitzer, heck, even Don Imus. Just make sure to bring bouncy shoes for jumping up and down on Oprah's couch.

Finally, wait until your misdeeds are forgotten, which, in American culture, will take about thirty-five minutes. Just don't make a big deal about it. Think of all the baseball players who, after being named in the Mitchell Report, 'fessed up, shrugged, and moved on. You can't think of them, can you? Because they're back at it, cheating themselves rich again.

# Conclusion

## You Got Rich Cheating!

Wow.

You did it. You are no longer poor. You're rich. *Exhale*.

You started with nothing; chose a profession; changed your body and your mindset; surrounded yourself with allies; blackmailed them; exploited employees; stole their pensions; used accounting tricks; stole your competitors' ideas and game plans; didn't pay taxes; used buddies to get government contracts; manipulated the media; deceived the public; bribed the refs; covered your tracks; bogged down prosecutors with legal mumbo jumbo; and managed to escape to a friendly country with tropical drinks and a whole new population just waiting to be had.

Congratulations. You Got Rich Cheating. *You're welcome*.

You made friends, you made enemies, but, most important, you made *money*. Lots and lots and lots and lots of

# Conclusion

money. Go buy yourself another baseball team or an island or pay to resolve an unrequited love. You deserve it.

You might have even come up with cheating ideas of your own. *Tell me.* The Great Cheaters count on you to discover new ways to Get Rich Cheating and expand our collective knowledge. Send me *your* Succe$tory. When I get enough, I'll put together a sequel. Guaranteed.*

---

\* Yes, guaranteed.

---

# Acknowledgments

A lot of time and effort went into this book, and countless people contributed to it and supported me in ways I can never truly repay. I'd like to thank a few by name:

My parents, Barbara and Michael, for birthing me, raising me, and providing more opportunities than I deserved.

Michelle Kreisler Rubenstein, for offering business insight and for protecting her little brother, even when literally spitting on him.

David Kreisler, for sacrificing vacations for a spoiled brat who didn't even know you were doing it.

Jack, Emma, Owen, Alison, Claire, and Jane, for being the little people.

Aaron Task, for chatting over Chinese food in San Francisco, suggesting the ridiculous idea of a business humor column, helping grow it, reading the first draft of this thing, and pretending said draft didn't suck.

CPQY, for inspiring and challenging me since 1991.

Bruce Cherry, for comedy insight and uninhibited positivity.

Joe Moore, for art.

Mary Bechmann, for research many moons ago.

Al Gore, for inventing the internet.

# Acknowledgments

Communitea, for allowing at least one neighborhood crazy to sulk and curse and occasionally write while nursing a small coffee.

The New York Public Library, for free workspace far from my refrigerator and e-mail.

The Universe, for not imploding before I finished.

Jim Boyd at Prentice Hall, for saying, "Hey, ever think of writing a book?" Even though it didn't work out, you got the ball rolling.

Jason Yarn at Paradigm, for picking up that ball after it ran over broken glass, then reinflating the ball, believing in the ball, telling a bunch of people how great the ball was, and helping guide the ball through the hoops. Also, for putting up with extended ball metaphors.

Matt Harper at HarperCollins (no relation), for seeing something in a book without a home, being willing to take a chance on it and a nobody author, and then shaping it into something special with incredible patience, insight, and humor. Everyone else at HarperCollins is pretty cool too.

Most of all, Anne, for saying, "Are you joking?" on a cold night in Madison Square Park . . . then following up with "Yes." For not changing your mind once the offer grew to include angst and confusion and worry. For climbing mountains. For focusing, inspiring, guiding, teaching, reading, rereading, laughing, fake-laughing, researching, asking, pushing, prodding, slapping, and, most of all, for loving. I have no idea why you do it, but I'm eternally grateful. I'd be empty without you.

CPSIA information can be obtained
at www.ICGtesting.com
Printed in the USA
LVHW030130270919
632410LV00003B/3/P

9 780061 686146